YOU WANT ME TO...
WHAT?

Risking Life Change to Answer God's Call

YOU WANT ME TO...
WHAT?

Risking Life Change to Answer God's Call

NORM GRANT

Seraphina Press
Minneapolis, MN

SERAPHINA
PRESS

Seraphina Press
212 3rd Avenue North, Suite 290
Minneapolis, MN 55401
612.455.2293
www.SeraphinaPress.com

ISBN - 978-0-9841965-1-7
ISBN - 0-9841965-1-x
LCCN - 2010922813

Cover Design and Typeset by Melanie Shellito

All Scripture quotations are from the following translations:

Scripture quotations marked (NIV) are taken from the *Holy Bible, New International Version®.*
NIV®. Copyright © 1973, 1978, 1984 by International Bible Society. Used by permission of
Zondervan. All rights reserved.

Scripture quotations marked (TNIV) are taken from the *Holy Bible, Today's New International
Version®. TNIV®.* Copyright © 2001, 2005 by International Bible Society. Used by permission of
Zondervan. All rights reserved.

Scripture quotations marked (NLT) are taken from the *Holy Bible, New Living Translation,*
Copyright © 1996. Used by permission of Tyndale House Publishers, Inc.,
Wheaton, Illinois 60189. All rights reserved.

Scripture quotations marked (AMP) are taken from the *Amplified® Bible,* Copyright © 1954, 1958,
1962, 1964, 1965, 1987 by The Lockman Foundation. Used by permission.

Scripture quotations marked (MSG) are taken from *The Message.* Copyright © 1993, 1994, 1995,
1996, 2000, 2001, 2002. Used by permission of NavPress Publishing Group.

Scripture quotations marked (NKJV) are taken from the *New King James Version.*
Copyright © 1982 by Thomas Nelson, Inc. Used by permission. All rights reserved.

Scripture quotations marked (NCV) are taken from the *New Century Version.*
Copyright © 2005 by Thomas Nelson, Inc. Used by permission. All rights reserved.

Scripture quotations marked (NASB) are taken from the *New American Standard Bible®,*
Copyright © 1960, 1962, 1963, 1968, 1971, 1972, 1973, 1975, 1977, 1995 by
The Lockman Foundation. Used by permission.

Internet addresses (websites, etc.) are offered as a resource to you and are not intended in any way
to be or imply an endorsement by the Publisher or Author, nor do we vouch for the content of
these sites for the life of this book.

Printed in the United States of America

What people are saying about this book:

"This book is inspiring. It definitely motivates me into action. It is a biography with valuable life and spiritual lessons. I loved it. Now I need to press in and seek His will for me."

— *Al De Simon, Executive Pastor*

"I love the way Norm's brand of humor weaved scripture masterfully into his personal and professional anecdotes! Life changing! A must read!"

— *Andy Harvey, Entrepreneur*

"Norm is a risk-taker, yet he takes risks for one purpose only — to glorify God and further His kingdom. In *You Want Me To ... What?,* Norm's message of risk, change, and obedience is one that is sorely needed by Christ's church today. Norm skilfully weaves personal stories with scriptural references and biblical interpretation to illustrate the need for God's people to strive for obedience. Christ's church is at stake! He challenges his readers to step out of the boat, to be courageous, to be risk-takers; however, this challenge is grounded in scripture and faith. The question is, will we — as a people and as a church — accept this challenge, right here ... right now?"

— *Heather Malnick, Pastor*

" I have been in Christian leadership for a couple of decades and have found this book both a timely read and a fresh wind (not breeze, that's too comfortable) reminding me to listen and not get stuck, to be continually stepping out of my comfort zone — where undoubtedly, Jesus is cheering us on. Thanks Norm — for 'not just sitting there!'"

— *Paul Simons, Church Army in Canada and National Director, Equipping Evangelists*

FOREWORD

Books come alive for us when we find ourselves in the story. The very best example of this is the Bible. It portrays God's story of redemption and hope. God invites us to find our place in His story through Jesus Christ. Norm has written a story that also invites the reader to find themselves in it. I am pleased to say that worked for me on many levels.

Firstly, I admit to being the one that left his car running for hours early in the book. I trust it alleviates some of your concern for our environment if you know it was a 2000 Volkswagen Jetta Diesel burning sulfur-free fuel.

But way more importantly, I found myself in Norm's story through the phrase *"You want me to... WHAT?"* as God has continued to surprise me year by year and even day by day. And in the greatest leaps of faith, as He stretches not just my self-imposed limitations but also my horizons and territories, I have found some of the greatest blessing and growth in my God relationship.

My hope and prayer is that Norm's story will provide you with much more than an entertaining look into his story but that it also be a vehicle for God to get your attention and response. May many lives be changed through the power of the Holy Spirit as people engage this book. Amen.

Fred Stewart, B.A., M.T.S., M.Div.
Pastor

ACKNOWLEDGEMENTS

This book is dedicated to Deb, Rob, and Kristina. Thank you for your loving support and encouragement while walking this journey with me.

TABLE OF CONTENTS

Chapter 1

"RIGHT HERE ... RIGHT NOW"

"Character isn't something you were born with and can't change, like your fingerprints. It's something you weren't born with and must take responsibility for forming." Jim Rohn

"Action is character." F. Scott Fitzgerald

"If we are faithless [do not believe and are untrue to Him], He remains true (faithful to His Word and His righteous character), for He cannot deny Himself." 2 Timothy 2:13 (AMP)

The calm quietness that had gently settled over the neighborhood was being shattered by my two-year-old son. He would repeat the phrase, "but Daddy I can't, I can't, I can't" as only an excited child can scream, in a way that gets everyone's attention. I kept cheering him on, telling him that it would be okay for him to jump into the water. But he's not jumping. With every reassurance he responds with the same phrase being repeated but growing louder and louder each time. His whole body is twitching with the excitement of wanting to jump in and experience something totally new but holding back and embracing the comforts of the nice dry deck surrounding the pool.

I know that I'm going to catch him. I know he's going to be just fine. I know that the experience of jumping into the pool for the first time will be exhilarating. I know, but he hasn't experienced it yet to know for himself. Oh, how I want him to just jump! It's a beautiful day and the sun is shining and the water is clear and as blue as the sky. The pool has been cleaned. In fact, there isn't a piece of dirt anywhere that would make a two-year-old decide not to jump in because it was "too dirty!" No, it's a great day and today, I hope, would be the day that my son was going to jump into the pool all by himself.

It took a long time to convince him that it was going to be worth the risk of doing this and there was nothing to worry about because I'd be there to catch him. I kept saying that it would be a blast and so much fun and he'd be able to splash me when he jumped in and we could see how big a splash he'd make. I even confirmed that I was sure that Batman does this all the time and if he wanted to be a superhero he'd have to eventually do the same thing and jump in.

"So big guy ... it might as well be today ... so what do you say you jump right now and let go of your fear and just jump?" I cheered. "Don't worry, I'll catch you," I promised. He didn't jump after that prompting, even though the Batman comment had him thinking.

Eventually, though, he did jump, and laughed and cheered and celebrated. Through this experience his perspective changed. He did experience everything that I told him he would, and once he risked stepping off of that ledge and letting go of his fear, his world changed. Once he had conquered it he kept wanting to do it over and over again. It was life changing for him, as it is for any of us when we find the strength and courage to risk doing something that we find intimating or insurmountable. He did it and he overcame the fear that was holding him back. His belief in himself grew. He was more confident around the pool and in the water. He was officially in training to become a superhero.

Now jump forward 12 years.

It's a beautiful day and the rocks of Georgian Bay are reflecting the sun's rays making it look like they're dancing with diamonds. The Georgian Bay area is magnificent. It truly is a wonder of the world where God created what some believe to be a small piece of heaven. The famous artists the Group of Seven journeyed this area getting their inspiration for their painting. It's that beautiful. I always feel closer to God after time spent in this area.

On this particular day the cliffs were calling and the group of us headed up the pathway to get to a spot on the cliff where there was a ledge about thirty feet above the water. It didn't look that high as we parked the boat on the nearby beach. Once docked it didn't take long for my son to be one of the first to lead the charge up the path. He was totally pumped with excitement at the adventure that lay ahead: to jump from a piece of rock and free-fall into clear dark blue water. He didn't even think about it. When he got to the ledge, he looked down, and before I could catch my breath from the steep climb to remind him of the day by the pool so many years ago, he was already risking it and jumping off. The quietness of that part of the bay was shattered with his joy-filled scream as he moved towards the water like a sleek missile cuts the air. Would he have reacted to this opportunity differently if in times past, like those around the pool, had he hadn't been encouraged to jump in? Perhaps.

I did manage to watch him jump while still trying desperately to catch my breath. Before long everyone who climbed up the cliff had jumped and it was just me standing there wondering what I had gotten myself into. Then before I knew it my son yells to me that I'll be okay and he'll catch me. That made me laugh. It brought back memories of me standing in the pool calling out to him. It helped cut my nervousness as I looked down at the small objects bobbing in the water below. "Just let go and jump, Dad. You can do it," he offered in an encouraging way. That helped a little bit, although it still didn't stop my knees from shaking. How quickly things change. Now it's me wanting to scream, "I can't," but instead I have to keep my composure; after all, I'm the adult, and somehow find the strength to let go of my fears and jump.

I did eventually jump. I'd like to tell you that I looked as graceful and sleek as a whale jumping up and cutting the ocean water. Some people who were there might agree that it looked like a whale, but graceful and sleek are not words that would be used to describe my entrance into the water. I risked. I jumped. I survived and my perspective was broadened. My confidence was elevated. My appreciation for dealing with fear and embracing risk was heightened. The experience was life changing. It was an absolute blast. A total rush.

What if God is the adult standing in the pool and He's calling out to us to risk jumping in? He knows full well that the experience will change our lives and that He'll catch us if we happen to struggle. I believe He's standing there calling out to each of us to jump and experience the life and adventure that awaits us when we respond to His calling. He tells us not to worry that He'll be there for us and if we fall he'll pick us up and put us back on our feet again. Yet, oftentimes we dance around the edge of the pool avoiding the invitation to risk life change by staying safe. Yes we really want to jump but instead we just scream out that "we can't Daddy" even though He gives us all the promises and assurances that we can and He will protect us. He just wants us to jump and experience something really amazing ... life change. Yet, despite all of His assurances, we miss out on way more than we participate in. We miss out on seeing things in a different perspective and one that is closer to how He sees us and our potential. We miss out on all of the experiences He has waiting for us by not letting go of our fears and just jumping into His arms. We miss out on risking life change.

What if God is doing that very thing to each of us right now. What if He's calling us to let go and risk real life change?

I'm reminded of the story of a person wandering down a path along the cliffs abutting the sea, each step taking him toward a new journey. It doesn't take long for him to become distracted, lose his footing and fall over the edge of the cliff. As he hangs on by his fingertips, his ability to fight the pull of gravity wanes with every shout for someone to help him. Time passes. How much time, he doesn't know. All he knows is that no one has responded and he fears that no one will respond. Desperation sinks in and, with his last ounce of energy, he calls out for someone to come and save him. "Please, is anyone out there who can help me? I can't hold on any longer!" He calls out until exhaustion starts to set in and he knows that he is down to his very last call for help. He has nothing left and is about to lose the battle to hold on. With no apparent response to the call, he relives the moments of his life, realizing all of the lost opportunities to really do something, to live a life awe-inspiring to others. That life is about to end. The only sound breaking through the stark realization is the sound of the waves crashing on the rocks below.

With one final desperate call, a plea, a final attempt to draw attention to his plight, he musters, "Is anyone out there who can help me?"

A very small voice responds with, "I can help you." That one response fills the fallen one with a new found enthusiasm.

"Oh, thank you for hearing my call! I've been hanging on for my dear life, here, and I don't think I can hang on much longer. Can you help me? Are you still there?"

"I am."

"Oh great! Hey, I can't see you. Where are you? Who are you?"

After a brief silence, the voice responds, "I am the Lord your God and I can help you."

"Oh wonderful. God, thank you for answering my call. I'm sorry I haven't lived a life that has been pleasing to you. I know I've made a lot of mistakes and, in fact, up until most recently ... well, like, as of before right now ... you weren't really part of my life. But as soon as you rescue me from this cliff I promise you that we'll spend a lot more time together. Can you just get me down from here, now? Please?"

God responds, "I'll rescue you, but you have to promise that you'll do everything I say to reach safety."

"I promise, God. From this day forward, I promise I'll do whatever you tell me to do, just get me off of this cliff."

"You'll do exactly as I say?"

Again, the person counters with, "Absolutely, I promise to do exactly as you tell me to do, so please rescue me, now."

"Then, let go."

"You want me to ... *WHAT*?!"

"You heard me. I want you to trust me and let go."

"But, I can't see you. I can hear you, but, God, I can't see you and what you're asking me to do is way too risky and outside of my comfort zone. Don't take this the wrong way as I'm positively sure that I want to get down from here without a scratch ... but ... I'm not certain that you'll catch me."

"But, I thought you promised that you'd do whatever I told you to do?"

"I did ... I know I did. But, what you're asking me to do doesn't make sense. Besides, how do I know that I can trust you?"

"Don't worry," God counters. "I won't drop the ball, so to speak, nor will I forget you or abandon you or fail you. I'll catch you by your right hand and lead you to safety. You know that this isn't the first time that I've called you to something like this."

"It's not?"

"No ... in fact I've called you many times, but you've either been distracted or you haven't wanted to hear me."

"I don't think I've ever heard you call me before, in fact I can't recall you ever calling me"

"Oh, I have many times. It's just that you heard me speak this time because there were no other distractions or options to your call for help. There have been many times before where you've heard me, but not wanted to acknowledge it."

"Hey, can we just skip the whole 'let go' thing and you rescue me and then we'll talk about how we can handle something in the future?"

"I think we should deal with this moment right here... right now. You know it's not like I'm asking you to do something that hasn't been done before. There have been lots of people throughout history who have been in similar situations to the one you're in right now and I've called them to do something that made absolutely no sense whatsoever."

"Yeah, but it's always easier to watch someone else go through something like this than actually do it yourself."

"Of course, it's always easier to watch than to act. Too many of my people do that, but for now this is your moment... right here... right now. Will you let go and trust me?"

After a very long pause the person cries out, "Is anyone else out there who can help me?"

* * * *

This response is so typical of us humans, isn't it?

Can you imagine what's going through this person's mind after hearing that call from God? How would you respond to such an illogical request? At that point in time nothing else in this person's world would matter because he'd be preoccupied with the two options before him. It is probably safe to say that he's not worried about the box scores to a particular game, what television shows will be on that evening, the most recent rumor winding its way through the neighborhood. Nor will he be worried about the next promotion, the next car, the dream home he's always wanted. No, at this point his only concern is how he's going to answer the call... right here... right now.

These "right here... right now" moments are monumental in this journey called life. They not only develop our character, but they also determine the path/journey we take and the type of experiences we have along the way. Right here ... right now moments are the catalysts to calling our character into action. How we respond to such moments not only provides us with opportunities to learn more about ourselves and who we are, but also opportunities for us to see the potential we have in God's eyes. Rick Warren says, "We won't take our career into eternity but we will take our character."

What would you do if you were hanging on by your fingertips? Every one of us can relate to a moment in our lives when we've made a wrong turn, stepped off the edge of a cliff and found ourselves totally exhausted, afraid and alone. We wait in desperation for someone to answer our plea, "Is there anyone out there who can help me?" Perhaps you know the decisions you've made that have brought you to this point in your life. Perhaps you never saw it coming, at all. At that moment in time, though, the past doesn't matter and you'll do anything to just have someone answer your plea for help and get you off that cliff. Perhaps you are there right now, experiencing some element of life that has left you clinging by your fingertips and calling out for someone to help you.

Maybe you're still stranded on that cliff, but have found a ledge that you can prop your foot on to relieve the pull of gravity, even for a short while. But you know that it's only temporary. Eventually reality/gravity will hit, and, with it, the stark realization that you can't hold on forever and you need someone to answer your call... right here... right now.

You might be one of the fortunate few on a path lined with gold, and life is moving along just fine. As you look to your left all you see is a horizon at the end of beautiful ocean with gentle rolling waves lapping the shore. To your right, as far as the eye can see, is beautiful green grass gently blowing in the wind where each blade of grass dances with sunbeams. Don't you worry. Sooner or later you will find yourself hanging from a cliff by your fingertips, calling for help.

In the story of the man hanging by his fingertips, we don't know how the story ends outside of man's typical response to God's call, and that response reflects our natural reluctance to fully embrace and trust God especially when things don't appear to make sense. What would happen if you were invited to write the ending of this story? Would you write it so that the one stranded would have heard God's instructions to "let go," and yet refuse to do so until someone else answers his call for help. Eventually his fingers would have given way a little at a time, inch by precious inch, until the person falls to his death. Maybe he would have been missed by the human race. Perhaps he would have garnered a sound bite on the local news. Maybe... maybe not. Yet no one would know of the one and only response to their call for help and the instruction to let go except the caller and the callee.

Perhaps you'd write the ending where someone else is walking along her very own path, minding her own business looking at the sea to her left and the green grass to her right, and hears a voice from above telling her to go closer to the edge. From deep within, a voice tells her to go left instead of straight. Right here... right now. And she comes across the person hanging from the cliff. She reaches out to help, the other reaches out in trust and as they work together, they step out of their respective comfort zones to accomplish something far greater than they could on their own. Perhaps in your ending, that desperate individual entrusts their life to this someone they could see, and then, once safe, the story would be told as to what prompted the called to go off the path and save the caller. They would recount the story many times and celebrate their part in the rescue amongst their small circle of friends, never really paying attention to how the hanging one denied God's call and how the rescuer was prompted to step off their well-organized and planned path. Perhaps, as they grew older, their kids would roll their eyes at every family gathering, at the "Let me tell you about the time when..." story, and the story dies with the teller.

Maybe, just maybe, the story would be told of how this person did let go and God caught him and brought him to safety. It would make for a wonderful story that would be repeated time and time again to as many people as would listen. Maybe those who heard the story would remember it when they found themselves hanging from a cliff with God calling them and decide to let go when He asked. Before you know it, other "rescue" stories would circulate the world, dominating Facebook pages, blogs, and websites. This type of outcome would have a huge impact on rescuees' understanding of who they are, what God is willing to do for each of them and others, and also who they are in God's eyes—worthy to be rescued by the active, living God. Collections of these stories of faith put into action would gain momentum and get passed on to the next generation. At every family gathering the next generation would beg the older one to tell them the story about how God told them to do the unthinkable and He rescued them. Then they would tell how as a result of someone witnessing the rescue or being told of the rescue, that person was influenced to do the same, and so on and so on. How inspiring would that ending be?

This story remains unfinished and it calls out to each of us to take hold of our pens and write its ending. To place ourselves on that cliff, hanging on for dear life, calling out for help, hearing God's call on our lives, and finish the story in our own unique way, based on our experiences. How would your story end? It would, no doubt, be different than mine and some would be far more dangerous than others. Maybe your story would be based on the dreams you have always had, but never found the strength to chase. Or, maybe they could be stitched in time when something so great and powerful happened that the lesson became the norm for your life. How would you write the ending to this "right here... right now" moment?

Our character is defined by how we view our past

experiences and how they shape our response to future "right here ... right now" moments. God calls each of us to participate with Him in the writing of such moments. Our response and the outcome to such moments are dictated by how we put our faith into action. It is written that "the fundamental fact of existence is that this trust in God, this faith, is the firm foundation under everything that makes life worth living. It's our handle on what we can't see. The act of faith is what distinguished our ancestors, set them above the crowd."[1] That's what this book is about: inspiring all of us to write about what happens when we "let go" and put our faith into action. People love to hear, live through, and participate in stories written out of right here... right now moments. There is no greater testimony to our character than those stories where God has called us to do something extraordinary, something that makes no sense whatsoever, and yet we let go and put our faith into action!

In turn, God answers our obedience to His call by catching us with His victorious right hand. In doing so, He answers the biggest questions that stir everyone's soul: Am I worthy of being rescued? Will you really save me if I let go? Will you catch me? If only we would let go when He calls. We're inspired by stories where God has done such a thing because all of us want to know that we are worthy of participating in something dangerous and exciting. Answering "the call of our Creator is 'the ultimate why' for living, the highest

---

[1] *The Message* Hebrews 11:1–2

source of purpose in human existence."[2] We want to know that we're called into something far bigger than ourselves, but the sad reality is the overwhelming majority of us miss such moments and never respond to God's call.

My hope in writing this book is to share part of the story that God has been writing in and through my life. His invitation to let go and risk life change. I pray that the Holy Spirit makes the words come alive for you and you'll be so inspired and touched by God's call for humanity to participate in the greatest adventure He has waiting for you that you will feel equipped and motivated to put your faith into action. That is of course if you will answer God's call on your life and call out to Him with the response "pick me." God has been calling us from the very beginning of time; calling us to put our faith into action thereby changing lives and contagiously inspiring witnesses. I hope you enjoy this book, that God's hand will be upon you as you read each page, that the Holy Spirit will surround you with wisdom, and that your ability to hear God's call will be exponentially heightened along with God-ordained boldness to take action... right here... right now!

---

[2] Os Guinness, *The Call—Finding and Fulfilling the Central Purpose of Your Life* (Nashville, TN: Word Publishing, 1998), 4.

Chapter 2

SOMEONE DO SOMETHING!

"Since Christianity is a faith that demands constant reflection and then change based on that reflection, we had better not get too comfortable." Rick Bundschuh

"And the LORD said to Samuel: "See, I am about to do something in Israel that will make the ears of everyone who hears of it tingle." 1 Samuel 3:11 (NIV)

A couple of months ago my wife, Deb, and I were out shopping. There was nothing extraordinary, different, or fancy about this particular day. Like everyone else, we were just trying to complete our to-do list for that day. The only exception being that it was just the two of us. The kids were at home. At one point during the day, we treated ourselves to a couple of those specialty coffees. You know, the ones served in a fancy cup with whip cream piled high and gently oozing over the edge of the cup? The ones that announce to everyone walking by that you're really cool and carefree in your approach to life and have free time on your hands. Well, that's what their marketing efforts want you to think. People watched us as we sauntered through the aisles just like the commercials for the coffee company said they would if we drank their coffee. It was unbelievable! Or, perhaps it was the blob of whip cream stuck to the edge of my nose that people were looking at.

In any event, this day we were given the gift of spending some time together; just the two of us, with no pressure to get the to-do list done by a certain time. It was just ... comfortable. We were oblivious to anything else outside the comfort zone and routine. It was fun just to be without any cares, deadlines, or other places to be. It turned out to be a very enjoyable afternoon and both of us remarked how thankful we were for this gift.

Everything changed in the blink of an eye when a voice rang out, "Help me! Help me! Someone do something, please!?"

Like a splash of cold water on your face first thing in the morning, our routine had been interrupted by a panic-stricken man a couple of feet away from us. As we looked in the direction of the call, our eyes confirmed what our ears had heard and our hearts had felt. It was not good.

A husband and wife had been doing exactly what Deb and I had been doing—trying to complete their to-do list. Perhaps the two were enjoying the freedom of an afternoon with no cares or obligations or other scheduled activities. Or, maybe they were totally stressed with all of the things on their to-do list and having to get somewhere else by a certain time, and the tension between the two was so thick it was about to shatter like concrete does when it meets a jackhammer. I'm not sure where they were at just moments before the husband's call echoed throughout the store, but I do know that things changed when people heard his call.

As we got closer, Deb's first-aid training kicked in and she, along with another lady, determined that the woman had had a seizure, collapsed, and had banged her head and was struggling to breathe. The husband was frozen in panic. The two women moved into action while the situation deteriorated quickly. The husband's panic was palpable and infectious, fueling his fear and desperation for someone to answer his call for help ... for someone to do something.

The two women took control of the situation. Within seconds, Deb had dialed 911 on her cell phone, handed the phone to the other lady to speak with the operator, then moved the injured lady onto her side so that she could breathe and would not be at risk of choking. They relayed to the operator what was happening and implemented the instructions they were given. The tight restricted area didn't allow for a lot of people to step in so I did the only thing I could—pray. What struck me in all of this was my mind's replaying of the husband's call for help—"someone do something." As I prayed, the Lord revealed to me the many different circles of reaction to the call to do something.

The most immediate circle were the two women, complete strangers, who were on the phone with emergency services and working together to help the fallen woman while comforting the husband. They were actively doing something. The husband obviously wanted to do so much more, but all he was equipped to do was to gently rub her back and speak lovingly to his wife, trying to sound as calm as possible even as his insides erupted with fear, panic, and desperation.

The next circle of reaction was the staff of the store who had gathered around the two women and watched while waiting for the store manager to come over. When the manager arrived, he called 911 and was told that a call had already come in and the ambulance had been dispatched. The staff not only acted slowly, but with an attitude of being not really sure what to do and clearly leaning towards avoidance rather than doing something. Perhaps it was fear that kept them from stepping in and responding to the call to do something or maybe they were reluctant to break out of their routines by answering the call. Regardless, their actions were contrary to what was called for. Someone needed to move quickly and take control, but they froze in fear unable or unwilling to fully respond to the call to do something.

The next circle of response comprised other shoppers who had heard the call, briefly stopped their to-do list to glance in our direction and realize there was a problem. They continued doing their own "something." Perhaps they felt that if they stayed far enough away from the situation they could justify not doing anything at all, thinking that no one would see their lack of response. I wondered how many others had followed suit.

Outside that circle was another, and perhaps the largest, group of all. They were the group who never heard a thing and continued on with their routine of comfort, totally oblivious to anything else going on around them.

In the midst of these circles of response, the paramedics arrived and took control of the situation. They had responded to the 911 call, assessed the situation, and taken action. Their answer to the call for help allowed us to step away from the situation. We tried to the best of our ability to step back into the moment we were before we heard the call. We tried, but it didn't last long as Deb and I both confessed that we didn't really feel like shopping anymore. We only wanted to leave, so we lined up at the checkout line, both of us not really saying too much to each other, but thinking a whole lot. We were hit with the stark realization of just how precious this phenomenal gift of life was and how quickly things could change. When our words broke the silence they spoke about how much we loved each other, our kids, our families and how appreciative we were for the precious time that we have here on earth.

As we left the store, we had to walk around the ambulance, which was parked at the front door with its lights flashing. It was parked in such a way that to get in or out of the store people had to alter their path and walk around it. People didn't miss a beat, and were not deterred in anyway except by a moment's curiosity about what was going on inside. Then they grabbed a shopping cart, opened up their "to-do" list and responded to the call of the list.

That's the cold hard fact about our human nature isn't it? The majority of people have become so hardened to the reality of just how precious this gift of life is that the call of the to-do list, the daily monotony of demands of keeping up with everybody else, blinds us to what we're missing out on. We're missing out on an entirely new perspective and world around us, a world that is calling out for someone to do something, something that matters, something that will affect and save lives, something that will rescue us from the day-to-day, same ol', daily routine and comfortable boredom that grinds all of us into a slow spiritual and physical death. Are you in that spot right now? Is the call of the to-do list so strong that you can't hear any other call on your life right now? Or, perhaps you've heard a call to do something and you've responded. If that's the case, I applaud you because the sad reality is the majority of people don't respond at all.

What if, instead of the husband, it was Jesus standing over his bride—the church—calling out for us to "do something"? What if He were calling us to participate with Him in regenerating and reviving our lives, His church, the country, and the world? What if He were calling us to step away from the comfortable routines and experience the amazing, the impossible, the God-ordained, life-transforming moments that He's longing to do in and through each of us? What if?

Some people never heard the call for help that day in the store and their routine continued as it always had. Perhaps they missed the call altogether and they're still searching for something to break them out of the noose of monotony that has formed around their necks, paralyzing them from participating in something out of their comfort zone and far greater than themselves. Perhaps they heard the call, but chose not to respond and instead just continued on with their to-do list, shutting down their internal receptivity to hearing any call at all. They've chosen for so many years to block these things out because it's always easier to not get involved. It's easier to not acknowledge and stay selfishly focused on themselves and their to-do list. Perhaps some heard the call and did nothing, but weren't able to let it go and God wrote this experience on their hearts so the next time they heard a call to do something they'd remember this moment and respond.

Does the routine of comfort block *our* ability to hear God calling *us*? I think it does. I'm reminded of the story about the time in our church history when things were really tough financially, the church was struggling to make ends meet, and it was not a very comfortable environment. Church leaders were concerned with the lack of resources and the constant struggle to be the church to the community around them. On one particular Sunday, Thomas Aquinas was counting the offerings for the day when an officer of the chancery walked in with a bag of gold collected in Absolutions and Indulgences. After the officer left, Pope Innocent III walked in and, when he looked upon the offerings, said to Aquinas, "You see, Thomas, the church can no longer say that gold and silver have I none." Implying that things would now be comfortably okay.

Aquinas replied, "Yes, Holy Father, but neither can she say rise and walk to the poor afflicted with palsy," implying that as a result the church would now lose the ability to hear God's prompting to participate in the miraculous.

Comfort and safety are frequency waves of interference that hinder our ability to hear God calling us to do something by stepping out of our daily routines of comfort. God is calling you and I ... right here ... right now. He has been since the beginning of time, is right now in the midst of our time, and will be in the future. That's His pattern. The Bible is the historical account of God pursuing His people to respond to His call.

So, if God is calling us to step out of our routine of comfort, how do we begin to hear that call? The Old and New

Testaments use several different words to refer to the word "call" and they are all verbs. Some make reference to drawing attention to oneself, preaching and proclaiming, naming, etc. In its basic context, the word call is used primarily to get people to do something. It's an invitation, a prompting by God, a right here ... right now moment that calls people to move from one point to another, and it involves four very distinct elements:

The caller: the one who initiates the action of calling with a very definite motivation to get someone's attention and invite them to do something;

The callee: the receptor of the initial invitation. The one who receives the invitation runs it through a complicated filtering system all the while processing the implications of receiving the invitation and what's going to happen if they act on or do not act on that invitation;

The response: Upon deliberation, the callee decides whether they'll accept or decline the invitation, or ignore it and pretend like nothing was ever received, even though deep down inside their heart will know that they heard it;

The result: Regardless of the actual response to the invitation, there is a result. It's irrefutable and undeniable. It could be something so extraordinary that people stop in awe of what they have just seen. Perhaps it's something deep inside us that dies as a result of ignoring the invitation and not responding, of staying dormant and lifeless.

The Sea of Galilee has lots of water coming into it from rivers and tributaries. Rather than holding on to that water, it releases it to other bodies of water. The water inside the

Sea of Galilee is constantly moving, changing, and adapting, and is one of the most vibrant bodies of water in the Middle East. The Dead Sea on the other hand receives the water from the Sea of Galilee, but because the water doesn't go anywhere outside itself it has no place to move and ends up being stagnant, stuck, and not moving at all. It is so totally full of salt that nothing can live in it, hence its name.

Consider for a moment the story of Peter and John as outlined in Acts 3:1–11:

> [1]One day Peter and John were going up to the temple at the time of prayer—at three in the afternoon. [2]Now a man crippled from birth was being carried to the temple gate called Beautiful, where he was put every day to beg from those going into the temple courts. [3]When he saw Peter and John about to enter, he asked them for money. [4]Peter looked straight at him, as did John. Then Peter said, "Look at us!" [5]So the man gave them his attention, expecting to get something from them. [6]Then Peter said, "Silver or gold I do not have, but what I have I give you. In the name of Jesus Christ of Nazareth, walk." [7]Taking him by the right hand, he helped him up, and instantly the man's feet and ankles became strong. [8]He jumped to his feet and began to walk. Then he went with them into the temple courts, walking and jumping, and praising God. [9]When all the people saw him walking and praising God, [10]they recognized

him as the same man who used to sit begging at
the temple gate called Beautiful, and they were
filled with wonder and amazement at what had
happened to him. (NIV)

Every day, this crippled man (the "caller") was carried
to the temple courts and called out for someone to do
something. Peter and John (the "callees") were following
their own routine of comfort. Part of their to-do list involved
going up to the temple for prayer every day, but they'd never
noticed this crippled man before. They'd never heard his call
for help. When they woke up that morning they had no idea
that God was going to break into their routine and call them
to do something. I love Peter's response when he says that
he has absolutely nothing of any worldly value to give. The
only thing he has to offer is an experience with the living
God. This is a right here ... right now moment.

There is, however, a deeper level to this circle of response,
and that is the power of the Holy Spirit which steps into our
daily routines and opens our ears to hear the call and our
eyes to see from where the call is coming. This would be a
day that God would open Peter's and John's ears to hear the
call to do something.[1] It's not like it hasn't happened before
to either Peter or John, especially while they were hanging
out with Jesus, but this day would be totally different from
any other.

Neither one of them responded with "You want me to ...
what?" and refused to move towards the crippled man. No,

---

[1] Proverbs 20:12 "Ears to hear and eyes to see—both are gifts from
the Lord." (NLT)

they moved towards the call and followed the prompting and awareness the Holy Spirit had stirred in them. The immediate circle of response was Peter, John, and the crippled man. They acted on the call to do something, and by linking into the name, power, and authority of Jesus Christ, a phenomenal response and healing occurred ... a miracle. There is, though, a larger circle of response to consider: those walking by on their way to the Temple who glanced at Peter and John and thought nothing more of it; those walking by who heard and saw nothing because they were totally focused on their own to-do list.

After the miracle, the three of them entered the Temple Courts celebrating what God had done, telling the story to everyone, including those who had just passed the crippled man as they entered the Temple that day. Everyone saw firsthand the result of answering God's call and so the larger circle of response was amazed at what had taken place. But I'm pretty sure they were questioning their lack of response and wondering if they had missed a life-changing experience with Yahweh. It's a great question and one that we should be asking ourselves every day.

I wonder if God was showing his church the need to step out of their routine of comfort and follow His promptings to experience powerful miracles. The funny thing here is that the miracle happens outside the Temple and the participants all go back into the Temple to tell others what has happened and then they join in celebrating what God has done. I wonder if that's one of the missing components to our Sunday routines in the church. Maybe we need to change our routine of comfort since "most churches are full of people who don't know how to look at what they are doing from another perspective, or they haven't been encouraged to try. If we're willing to stop merely talking about how big our God is and start experiencing His wonder and wildness, we're going to have to learn a few things."[2] So, what did those in the Temple learn that day from Peter's and John's response to the right here ... right now moment? Perhaps we need to celebrate more the miracles that God has done through us when we answer His call to do something; our time in worship should be more celebratory at what God has done the previous week and what He promises to do in the upcoming weeks when we answer His call.[3]

We need to be aware of the call, an invitation to experience a right here ... right now moment then we need to take responsibility and acknowledge the call to do something.

In 1983, an 11-year-old boy and his family's routine of comfort every night included watching the six o'clock news in their suburban Philadelphia home. One particular winter night, a code blue had gone out on the news to let people know that it would be an extremely cold night. Code blues also meant that there would be great strain on the downtown shelters as there were too many homeless people for the available beds. The call for someone to do something went out.

Trevor Ferrell heard the call and felt the prompting to act, so he pestered his family that night to take him downtown and let him give a blanket to the homeless man he saw on

---

[2] Rick Bundschuh, *Don't Rock the Boat Capsize It—Loving the Church Too Much to Leave It the Way It Is* (Colorado Springs: NavPress, 2005) 30.

[3] Revelation 2:7 "Anyone with ears to hear must listen to the Spirit and understand what he is saying to the churches." (NLT)

the news. He thought that it was only one man that needed to be helped so he kept after his parents to take him to see the one homeless man. They relented and took him down knowing that their son would soon have a huge awakening at the growing social need in their city. Trevor, overwhelmed by the number of people without any shelter that night, still delivers one small blanket to one of the homeless people. He repeated the same pattern every night afterward except the blankets soon grew into clothes and then warm meals all being prepared and coordinated from their comfortable suburban home, then delivered to those in need. Word spread about his efforts and soon churches and others jumped in answering the call to do something.[4]

Dietrich Bonheoffer says, "action springs not from thought but from a readiness for responsibility." Trevor's life-changing actions were initiated when he became aware of the call, then acknowledged the prompting that he was being called to do something.

After we have become aware of the prompting and acknowledged that something outside of ourselves is happening, we then must decide to either risk taking action or settle for the nagging feeling that we're missing out on something in our lives. Do we stay stuck in incompleteness or participate in and witness the evidence of God.[5] Trevor

---

[4] http://www.citypaper.net/articles/2003-12-04 accessed on 02/26/2009

[5] Isaiah 55:12 "So you'll go out in joy, you'll be led into a whole and complete life. The mountains and hills will lead the parade, bursting with song. All the trees of the forest will join the procession, exuberant with applause. No more thistles, but giant sequoias, no more thorn bushes, but stately pines—Monuments to me, to God, living and lasting evidence of God." *The Message.*

risked doing something. He let go and trusted God, and God honored his actions by exponentially multiplying his one small blanket into far greater results of life change than even Trevor expected. That one blanket turned into a charity that has helped thousands of lives, all because he put his faith into action and risked doing something.

The Book of James outlines the key to living a complete life and it's one of the key components to our understanding the essence of God's call for us to do something:

> "Suppose a brother or sister is without clothes and daily food. If one of you says to him, 'Go, I wish you well; keep warm and well fed,' but does nothing about his physical needs, what good is it? In the same way, faith by itself, if it is not accompanied by action, is dead. But someone will say, 'You have faith; I have deeds.' Show me your faith without deeds, and I will show you my faith by what I do. You believe that there is one God. Good! Even the demons believe that—and shudder. You foolish man, do you want evidence that faith without deeds is useless? Was not our ancestor Abraham considered righteous for what he did when he offered his son Isaac on the altar? You see that his faith and his actions were working together, and his faith was made complete by what he did." James 2:15–22 (NIV)

Okay, so now you're asking yourself, He can't be serious, can He? Would God actually be calling me to do something totally out-there, radical, wild and crazy? Doesn't He know that I'm too old, too tall, too short, too overweight, too skinny, too—you fill in the blank with your greatest excuse for why God couldn't use you like He used Peter and Trevor. Responding to and understanding the essence of God's call on our lives "is less about our comfort than it is about our contribution. God would never choose for us safety at the cost of significance. God created you so that your life would count, not so that you could count the days of your life."[6] How we measure the significance of our lives is in our response to right here ... right now moments and whatever excuses we attempt to hide behind are challenged by the powerful stories of those who answered God's call not with trepidation or fear, but with an excited, "You want me to ... *what?*"

Consider the story of Mary Clarke[7] (aka Mother Antonia). Mary Clarke lived in San Diego, going through the routines of a comfortable life. She had been divorced once and remarried, raised seven children, was running a business that her father had passed on to her, and doing the regular church thing at her local Catholic church. Yet, in the midst of this normal and comfortable life she felt like something was missing. The restlessness didn't go away until one day her husband suggested that she could collect clothing, shoes, and medicine for orphans in Korea. She followed the prompting and started to do just that. Within two to three

---

[6] Erwin Raphael McManus, *The Barbarian Way* (Nashville, TN: Thomas Nelson Inc, 2005), 44–45.

[7] Mary Jordan and Kevin Sullivan, *The Prison Angel: Mother Antonia's Journey From Beverly Hills to a Life of Service in a Mexican Jail* (New York, NY: Penguin Press, 2005)

years, she became very well known in the area as a powerful agent of change in the social justice scene in San Diego, which eventually led her to being invited to spend a day at the Le Mesa prison in Tijuana, Mexico, the toughest prison around.

On that visit, the Holy Spirit prompted her and God called her to spend the rest of her life there. She used her established contacts in the San Diego business community to help send food, dentists, and doctors to assist the inmates and to reach these inmates with the love of God. By this point, though, her husband decided that he'd had enough and they divorced. Her kids are grown. It was under these circumstances that God called her to do something totally opposite to her routine of comfort and make the prison her full-time ministry. She approached the Catholic Church about becoming a nun. They told her that she doesn't fit with what they're looking for as she's too old (50 years) and twice divorced. But that rejection didn't stop her. She decided to become an independent sister, making her own outfit to look "nunny" enough.

She sold her house, shut down the business and moved into the prison full-time. Literally! The Warden eventually provided her with her own ten-by-ten-foot cell where thirty-plus years later she still lives, today, helping the inmates to come into an experience with the loving God. God has powerfully used this lady to touch not only the prison community, but the surrounding areas, as well. She set up a hospice for the families of sick inmates so they could spend their last block of time together. She created an endowment fund for families of police officers who have been killed in the line of duty. And these are just some of the outcomes that have resulted by her reaction to the call.

Her awareness of God's call and willingness to follow the promptings of the Holy Spirit even though it meant risking her own life and doing something that made no sense whatsoever is foundational to right here ... right now moments. Her efforts have changed lives and impacted eternity. She's making the world a better place by answering the cry for someone to do something. Not only has she created her own sisterhood for women who are over the age of forty-five, which also has now been recognized by the Catholic Church, but her story has prompted other women to join her in the prison. These women have been motivated and inspired by Mother Antonia and they, too, have heard the call to do something.

We're never too old, too poor, too rich, too small, etc., to not respond to the call. The real questions are, how is God trying to get your attention, what is He calling you to do, and how are you going to respond?

Chapter 3

"YOU WANT ME TO ... WHAT?"

"This is what God says ...
"Forget about what's happened;
don't keep going over old history.
Be alert, be present. I'm about to do something brand-new.
It's bursting out! Don't you see it?
There it is! I'm making a road through the desert,
rivers in the badlands."
Isaiah 43:16, 18-19 *The Message*

At the time of Isaiah's message to the Israelites they were in exile. They had watched the decimation of their homeland, been forcibly dragged into foreign territory with nothing but the clothes on their backs, to live the rest of their lives oppressed by a despised enemy—Babylon. God used Isaiah to call to His people to pay attention because He was going to change things. Despite their current situation and regardless of what had happened in the past, their God—Yahweh—was about to do a brand new thing in their lives. God promised that despite how bad things looked, He would do the impossible and call all of them back to their homeland.

Through Isaiah, God told the people who their leader would be when this event finally happened. Cyrus wasn't even in power, yet, but God made His message very simple to understand and the signs of His plan easy to watch for so there would be no misunderstanding or chance of missing the call. God said that He would choose to do such a thing and even though the people would think it was totally impossible given their particular circumstances, it was going to happen and they needed to pay attention or they'd miss out.[1] This message is a call to action. A right here ... right now moment was coming, and through this moment, God was going to invite all of them to experience His mighty power first-hand.

By this time, thousands of Israelites had adjusted to this new life within the Persian Empire. It hadn't been easy for some, yet others had gone about their day-to-day lives and become very successful in this new land. They had established for themselves a routine of comfort. Some had forgotten about the long-standing covenant that one day God was going to call them back to their homeland, and others had not.[2] So, what do you think their response was to hearing the prophet Isaiah warning them that God was about to do something brand new and call them home?

For sure, some ignored the call. Others responded with "You want me to ... *what*?" in a pained, exasperated, you've-got-to-be-kidding tone. There were probably those who argued, "You can't be serious. The kids have adjusted to

---

[1] Isaiah 44:26–28 "But I carry out the predictions of my prophets! By them I say to Jerusalem, 'People will live here again,' and to the towns of Judah, 'You will be rebuilt; I will restore all your ruins! 'When I speak to the rivers and say, 'Dry up!' they will be dry. When I say of Cyrus, 'He is my shepherd,' he will certainly do as I say. He will command, 'Rebuild Jerusalem'; he will say, 'Restore the Temple.'" (NLT)

[2] Jeremiah 29:10 — This is what the LORD says: "You will be in Babylon for seventy years. But then I will come and do for you all the good things I have promised, and I will bring you home again." (NLT)

all the new schools and made friends, the new job is going just fine. We love our house, in fact, we just redecorated last month, we know where everything is and we're comfortable now after you uprooted us last time, and now you're calling us through this Isaiah fellow that you're going to do something brand new, something that makes no sense at all and you want me to get ready? You want me to ... *what?*"

Others who heard Isaiah speak those same words reacted totally differently. Those were the ones who had never forgotten the Lord's promises to deliver them. Their response was, "You want me to ... *what?*" in an excited, can't-wait-to-see-what-happens-next tone. They knew and believed that God was going to do something really big and they wanted to be ready for that moment when He called them back home.

In either scenario, God had called his people to pay attention as they were about to experience a right here ... right now moment. A call to do something so far out there and against all odds and in total disregard for human limitations that it would change their lives forever. Unfortunately, when the event actually happened, most of the people opted for the routine of comfort and staying put rather than going back home.

Don't let me stay comfy

How would you respond, today, if God called you to get ready for Him to do something brand new?

In our Bible story, God called someone outside of the Israelite family to be His vessel for facilitating the Israelites' migration to restore the Temple in their homeland: Cyrus, the pagan leader who would later be responsible for founding the Great Persian Empire, who would overthrow Babylon, and who would let the Israelites go back to their homeland.

God called a non-Israelite, a non-believer, to participate in His really big, brand new master plan. The Bible says that God stirred the heart of Cyrus to put this proclamation in writing and to send it throughout his kingdom: "This is what King Cyrus of Persia says: 'The Lord, the God of heaven, has given me all the kingdoms of the earth. He has appointed me to build him a Temple at Jerusalem, which is in Judah. Any of you who are the Lord's people may go there for this task. And may the Lord your God be with you!'"[3]

Cyrus would be God's catalyst to a special activity and he would be anointed by God for a special purpose—a "right here ... right now" moment—even though Cyrus had no current or past relationship with God. God can call anyone to participate in heavenly accomplishments and this is exactly what happened to Cyrus.

He was the key figure in founding the Great Persian Empire that "at its height stretched from Greece in the west to India in the east."[4] Cyrus was a definite powerbroker, a mover and shaker, and someone whose power and reach had great impact throughout the known world. He had no relationship with Israel's God, Yahweh. He, in fact, followed Marduk, the god of Babylon. So, when Yahweh used the prophet Isaiah to get the Israelites' attention that something new was going to happen, that brand new thing included Cyrus. He stirred Cyrus' spirit that something was going to happen to the Israelites, even though He knew Cyrus would

---

[3] 2 Chronicles 36:22–23 (NLT)

[4] Paul J. Achtemeier, General Editor, *The HarperCollins Bible Dictionary*, (San Francisco, CA: HarperSan Francisco, 1996), 832.

not point to Him—Yahweh—as being the author of that call to let the people go. Written on the famous cylinder of Cyrus, he gives credit for everything to his god, Marduk.[5]

Oftentimes, people mistake God's calling to participate in a right here ... right now moment as being from some other "god" in their lives when, in reality, it is the one and only God that is stirring their spirit to do a brand new thing. You may be experiencing a moment just like that right now in your own life. Or, perhaps you're looking back on some key life experiences where you can see how the working hand of the living God has been orchestrating some new and great experiences at a time when you had no reason to know or acknowledge God was calling you into a brand new experience.

I can look back on my first right here ... right now moment and know that it was God calling me to do something brand new, but at the moment it happened there were many different gods in my life—power, success, money—that blinded me from seeing the truthful source of the call. Call them the big three if you want (and, no, it's got nothing to do with car manufacturers), but they were the gods that controlled my life.

I've always been entrepreneurial and have had a strong calling, if you will, to achieve power, success, and lots of money. That type of calling is very typical in our Western culture, isn't it? Upon graduation from University in 1985, I started my career with the largest commercial real estate brokerage company in the world. If you say that fast enough

5   R.K. Harrison, editor, *The New Unger's Bible Dictionary,* (Chicago, IL: Moody Press, 1985), 270.

it can sound pretty impressive, can't it? I passed their detailed aptitude test and after many interviews I was offered a sales position in their downtown Toronto office. On my very first day on the job they handed me a manual and said, "We've been in operation for many years and this manual is the culmination of our learning during those years of experience in providing people with the foundation for lots of successful results"—think $$$$ here—"and so if you do everything that we say in this manual, everything, you will achieve these types of results." So I opened up the big binder and began reading their plan for my life.

I started looking at it and thinking, "Wow, this is pretty easy to follow and if I just do as they say and follow their game plan just as it's laid out, I'm going to achieve power, success and money." So, that's what I did. I went to work thinking that if this manual were truly the benchmark of how and what to do during the week, then if I worked that much harder I would achieve those things sooner. I started to work seven days a week. I wasn't married at the time. I didn't have all of my high school buddies or university buddies around. My social circle had really become my business circle and my life became my business. My effort and the company's manual provided the necessary ingredients for results and gradually over a period of time, I hit every level of success outlined in the manual.

At the beginning of every New Year, the company would hold a special sales meeting over and above the normal weekly one to celebrate what had been accomplished in the year before, and to review where we had been and where we had finished for the year past. It was a way to see how we had done, but also a definite way to see our successes and set out new sales targets that would keep us motivated to achieve results in the upcoming year. Management would always ask how we could hit higher sales targets in the coming year, how we could improve, become better and more successful both corporately and individually.

Does this sound something like your world, right now? This mentality is ingrained in our culture. It doesn't matter what business or organization you work for, the reality is that come the beginning of every New Year, the slate is clean and you start at zero. It's implied, and accepted, that what you did last year wasn't good enough. You can always do better, and after a period of time you start to believe that to be somebody, to be significant, successful, powerful, and of worth, you have to hit that next milestone or you're not going to be good enough and you'll lose whatever status you achieved the previous year. You'll become a nobody. Have you ever been told that in your life? If you were really honest with yourself, you'd admit that at some point you had been told that.

So, every year my gods called me to push myself even harder so I didn't lose my status within the company, business community, etc., so I continued to work extremely hard and hit threshold after threshold and became, at that time, the youngest vice president of the Canadian company. So, there I was a vice president and really enjoying my all-consuming life. I was making more money than I had ever thought possible, I was going on President Club performance trips to wonderful locations only offered to those who met certain financial thresholds during the year. I had met this beautiful and wonderful girl, who I ended up marrying, and am still married to her. Thankfully, she's a very kind and patient lady. I was in tune with my gods as my life's status and success was reflected in trophies, expensive suits, sports cars, memberships at exclusive private golf clubs, and a golf game to match the status of the club. I had no concern for what a meal was going to cost. I had in essence achieved the status that I sought out to achieve when I first read through that manual.

Perhaps it was boredom, sheer competitiveness of being in a full commission business or just the need to get noticed that prompted me one day in a meeting with my manager to ask the question, "What's next?" I guess the implied assumption put out every New Year had sunk in. I'm not good enough the way I am and I need to get better so, What's next? I wanted to know what my next challenge was so that my status, significance, worth, and inner need for acceptance from the world around me—a need to have the world take notice of me—would be met and I would be a somebody worth noticing.

My manager put a challenge out to me to make in one single commission deal more money than I had made in a year. That was a bold challenge, but one I thought could be met. It would require me to work harder and smarter than I had in the past. So, I went about it to get the check and was successful. I remember thinking to myself, *This is it. I've already achieved a lot, but with this check I'm going to get to that next level of significance, importance, and self-worth.*

I'm really going to be somebody now! I started to picture me receiving the check and I thought I would have this feeling of total elation when I deposited that check into my bank account and I saw that entry and resulting balance on my bank statement.

The day I received the check, I went over to the Bank of Montreal at the corner of King and Bay Streets in downtown Toronto and deposited the check. I remember walking out of the bank and standing at the corner and thinking to myself as I looked at that piece of paper, *Okay. That feeling I'm looking for is going to hit me soon.* I waited. And waited. But I felt nothing! You know that feeling when you get in an elevator and you push the button to go down and just at that moment your stomach goes, *Whoop*? That's the feeling I felt as I stood on that corner. People walked by me in slow motion and fast motion and I heard bits of conversations. It was surreal, like an out-of-body experience. It was the beginning of a right here ... right now moment and I knew that I was in trouble. It was right then that I realized if everything I had been told, bought into and believed in had been true, then I shouldn't feel this way. So that meant that if I felt this way, now, everything I had believed in and pursued must not be true. I had bought into a system and a dream and a format that had given me more than I had ever imagined, and yet I realized that I was in trouble and in desperate need of help.

I had been taught that I had total control over my destiny and future, and since I had created who I was, then surely I could solve this problem of why I felt like there was a gigantic hole in the center of me. My bearings on where and who I was had turned into a Swiss cheese of uncertainty. As the old saying goes, A self-made man worships his creator ... himself; and that self-worship had led me into this situation and I was lost. Now, I was a typical male. I was in trouble and I was lost, but I wasn't going to ask for directions. To do so would make me appear weak, vulnerable, and really lost. It's in these moments that God invites us to ask Him for direction all the time.[6] So, I started searching for the reason why I felt this way. I had this void in my life—a deep emptiness that challenged me to examine everything in my life to find out why this hole existed and what I needed to do to fill it.

Now, I never considered going to the church or seeking God to find the answers I was looking for. Our family had seasons of attending church. But I got to the age where I looked at the church and decided I had some issues and problems with the way they did things. On any given Sunday, a guy wearing a robe would stand above everyone, talk down to everyone, and whoever was outside of the church wasn't living a life the church would necessarily want.

On those days when we did make an appearance, the first thing I did was look at the hymn board. If there were two hymns on that hymn board each with one or two verses in them, then it was going to be a good Sunday because we were going to get out of there in less than an hour. But if that hymn board had five hymns and each one of those hymns had seven verses, I knew it was going to be a very long and

---

[6] Jeremiah 6:16 "This is what the Lord says: "Stand at the crossroads and look; ask for the ancient paths, ask where the good way is, and walk in it, and you will find rest for your souls." (NIV)

painful Sunday morning. Then, they plugged in the organ and started wailing away with a sound that screamed "danger ... danger ... these notes being played are unsuitable for human ears and if you listened long enough you'd swear that it all sounded like fingernails being dragged down a chalkboard. The church was full of hypocrites and their message had no bearing on my life.

So, the church was never a viable consideration or pathway for guiding me towards finding what I was missing. In fact, my business experience had taught me that the rule of thumb in dealing with religious clients was that you had to really watch your back because the more religious an individual/client you were dealing with the more you had to cover all of the angles since Monday to Friday they could do whatever they wanted, while Saturday and Sunday they could go to their respective synagogue or church, get forgiveness, and on Monday start all over. There was no reason for me to look towards the church, or God, as part of my solution.

So, I went about searching for answers by pursuing all the self-help books I could find. I became a self-help guru. I read books and listened to tapes on everything I thought could possibly give me an answer to fill this deepening darkening pit inside my stomach. You name it ... I read it. I was searching for why I felt this way and was seeking to understand what was happening to me. It started to impact my real estate career as the consistent upward trend of a growing income had now started to drastically decline. I quickly realized that this company, as good as it was, wasn't going to help me find what was missing from my life. They weren't going to provide anything for me. The real estate game is probably like a lot of other games out there asking, What have you done for me lately and how are you going to help achieve better results? If you provide something on either of those issues then the business world has time for you. If you can't, forget it. It just skips you by. That's the secular agenda. And sometimes that might even be the agenda of the church. But that's not the way Jesus had envisioned it.

Looking back on it, now, I realize that God was calling me and trying to get my attention. I knew that wherever this quest was going to take me that I would continue with it even if I was afraid of not knowing what was going on or why it was happening to me. On the one hand, I was excited that something new was bursting out inside of me. On the other hand, I was terribly afraid that I would no longer be a somebody, and I knew that this was an important moment in my life that I could not ignore. I made the decision to follow it without knowing what lay ahead. I had heard the call, but I wasn't sure of its source. This was a right here ... right now moment and, while I didn't realize it at the time, I now know beyond a shadow of a doubt that God was trying to get a hold of me and call me into new territory. His call was starting to stir my spirit.

I think Cyrus had a similar experience when God called him to do something totally brand new and, while he didn't necessarily have the correct source for everything that had happened during his rule of the Persian Empire he was nonetheless a different person as a result of God's calling. Perhaps there was a day in Cyrus' life when he looked back at the whole experience and knew that he was part of something far bigger than his empire. Where the stirring of his spirit led others to many blessings including letting the Israelites go back to their homeland and eventually rebuild their Temple. Perhaps in a dark quiet moment after his reign had ended, Cyrus realized that his god, Marduk, in fact had nothing to do with how it all went down and there was in fact only one true God that had called Cyrus to do something. The Bible says that the Lord stirred up the spirit of Cyrus of Persia[7] and God did this even though Cyrus was not a follower or even aware that God orchestrated it.

Right here ... right now moments are characterized by events in our lives that stir our spirits. They make us aware that something far bigger than ourselves is happening and we're being invited into it. It's opposite to what we expect and lies beyond the realm of the impossible. It smashes the routine of our daily lives and pays no attention to the status quo. It changes people's lives and impacts others around them. It pays no heed to the calling of comfort and takes us out into brand new uncharted territories. It focuses and invigorates our souls and, while we might not be able to name the source of the stirring at that particular moment, we know with a deep anchored certainty, that something brand new is about to happen and we're being invited to participate in it. This is where God enters ours lives and calls our attention to the impossible becoming possible, to him acting on our behalf and clearing a new way for us to travel

---

[7]   2 Chronicles 36:22 " ... the Lord stirred up the spirit of Cyrus ... " (AMP)

("There it is, it's bursting out. Don't you see it?"[8]), and our souls are stirred by something outside of our predisposed understanding of how things should be. We can't name it at the time, we just know that we have a choice: follow it and see where it leads or ignore it and lead a wasted life.

Is there a stirring going on in your life right now? Or, can you think of a time when such a thing happened to you and you ignored it? If the living God called you right here ... right now to an anointed and awakened opportunity that made no sense whatsoever, but you just knew that it was going to be a defining moment in your family, life, career, and calling ... how would you answer? Would your response be a painful, how-dare-you-ask, this-is-going-to-be-stupid, "You want me to ... *what*?" Or, would your response be an excited and enthusiastic, welcoming, I-can't-wait-to-see-what's-next, drop-everything-and-let's-get-going, "You want me to ... *what*?" Or, would you choose to ignore the call all together?

---

8   Isaiah 43:18 *The Message*

Chapter 4

THE SEARCH CONTINUES

"Rarely does our journey through life follow a straight and clear path from beginning to end." Jerry Sittser

"In his heart a man plans his course, but the LORD determines his steps." Proverbs 16:9 (NIV)

There's a very popular song written by the rock band U2 entitled, "I Still Haven't Found What I'm Looking For." The title says it all. Someone has been looking for something, but they still haven't found what they're looking for. It speaks about reaching the tops of mountains in success and life achievements, yet despite all of the songwriter's accomplishments he still hasn't found what it is that his heart really needs. The irony here is that at the time of writing this book, the band itself is known as the most popular, successful, and influential group in the entire music industry.

The song speaks of the call for our human spirit to find its purpose and meaning in life. Eventually we realize that meaning and purpose in life has nothing to do with material possessions or worldly accolades, and does, in fact, have everything to do with responding to the restlessness that occurs when we have achieved everything we thought we needed to achieve and yet still feel like something's missing. Despite everything we have there's still a quantum hole in the middle of our being that is calling our souls to focus on the need to feel complete. This stirring is God calling us to pay attention.

When He created each of us He formed our human spirit and planted deep within us[1] a longing that can only be filled with companionship with Him. God knows that we'll all reach a point where we long for the missing piece, which happens when our souls are stirred, and that we'll find what we're looking for when we start to look for Him. The Bible says "the Lord [earnestly] waits [expecting, looking, and longing] to be gracious to you; and, therefore, He lifts Himself up, that He may have mercy on you and show loving-kindness to you. For the Lord is a God of justice. Blessed (happy, fortunate, to be envied) are all those who [earnestly] wait for Him, who expect and look and long for Him [for His victory, His favor, His love, His peace, His joy, and His matchless, unbroken companionship]!" Isaiah 30:18 (AMP).

In my own case, I had cashed the check, but still hadn't found what I was looking for. All I knew was that my spirit had been stirred and my search to find the cause continued until one Friday night, Deb and I were debating over a movie to rent—okay, maybe we were passionately discussing the different options to watch. We each had well defined differences of opinion over which video to get. Who do you think won? Right, she picked a video and the debate was over.

Can you picture the routine of a Friday night, or any night for that matter, in any video store throughout the country?

---

[1] Zechariah 12:1 "This message is from the Lord, who stretched out the heavens, laid the foundations of the earth, and formed the human spirit." (NLT)

People aimlessly wander the aisles of the store looking for a video that will be entertaining and will have some meaning and impact for their lives. We all do this, some more so than others, but it happens all the time. We were just another couple walking around a video store looking for something that would have meaning and enjoyment for that evening and all the while the script of the invitation to pick the video had already been written. God had that moment ordained in time long before it happened and while at the moment it happened I viewed it as a coincidence, I realize now that there are no such things as coincidences, just moments of opportunity to explore and respond to God's many different ways He calls to our souls to get our attention.[2]

We ended up choosing *Mr. Holland's Opus*, a story about a high school music teacher who had a dream of writing one piece of music that would make him famous. For thirty years he toils away as a music teacher, seeing that job as a way of merely paying the bills until he completes the piece of music that would take him off to Broadway, riches, and world-acknowledgement. The movie spoke very powerfully to me about the significance and need to follow your dreams.

My dream was to own a golf course. I toyed with the idea of going pro, and then the comforts of the good life kept me from giving it all up to travel around the highways and byways in search of the next tin cup moment. Not to mention the fact that I now had others in my life to think about and I knew that trying to go pro would mean a very unstable

---

[2] Isaiah 49:8 "This is what the LORD says: "At just the right time, I will respond to you." (NLT)

family life. However, owning a golf course would in fact be the best of both worlds because it would keep all of us together and give me the dream. What's your dream?

Anyway, at the conclusion of the movie I looked over at Deb and I said that I didn't want to miss out on not realizing the dream. So, we went out the very next day and started searching for places where we could build our dream. Let's be fair, my dream. My wife is very understanding, did I tell you that? I had a strong hunch that this stirring toward finding the dream was perhaps the beginning of solving the quandary of the emptiness and giant hole in the core of my being, the one that had grown since depositing the check. So, we searched and searched and ended up moving north of Toronto into a beautiful resort area (Horseshoe Valley). We sold our house in Toronto and thought we'd try it for a year and if we didn't like it we could always move back. We hoped to either find a golf course to buy or some land that we could buy and build a golf course, but either way we'd build a field of dreams. I knew that this was a key moment in getting closer to whatever I was looking for, the deeper meaning of who I was, the need to find something that would fill the hole within me, the search for purpose and meaning by way of the dream. This was the time to begin searching.[3]

God calls to us through these moments where we begin the searching for the why behind the stirring of our spirits. At times, we think that we're actually controlling the whole process, when there is in fact a greater symphony of heavenly

---

[3] Ecclesiastes 3:1, 6 "For everything there is a season, a time for every activity under heaven ... a time to search" (NLT)

elements trying to get our attention through right here ... right now moments. In fact, long "before we first heard of Christ and got our hopes up, he had his eye on us, had designs on us for glorious living, part of the overall purpose he is working out in everything and everyone."[4] Again, at this key moment, God was writing on my soul, but I had no idea that it was Him. God was calling me to journey down a path that would not only change my whole world, but provide me with the answer I was looking for. All I knew at that moment, though, was that this movie had stirred my heart and called me to search for my dream.

So, being absolutely sure that my next step in this journey involved the opportunity to experience the dream of building/ owning a golf course, and even though I couldn't see the specific place or location of the golf course, I was completely certain that my own abilities could make it happen, and by taking the next step I was convinced that my calling in life would be found by securing the dream. Eventually, we adjusted to the new surroundings and became involved in the many different activities. Our son began kindergarten and we enrolled our daughter in a Christian-based daycare located a couple blocks away from our house. We placed her there for no other reason than it was an awesome daycare program that was really convenient and we just had a great feeling about the lady that ran it. Little did we realize the impact that this small little daycare and the woman who ran it would have on our family. Deb continued her teaching career in a new school board and I continued with my real estate while searching for

4   Ephesians 1:11 – *The Message*

the right opportunity for the dream. Life was good and it felt like we were making progress.

Then, one night after dinner, Deb and I were going through the mail and we noticed a flyer from this new church starting up in the area inviting us to join them on the upcoming Sunday. We didn't give it any thought and Deb immediately put it in the pile slated for the garbage. It's not that we had anything against church ... well, other than it was boring, irrelevant, full of hypocrites, had lousy music and was basically a total waste of time especially on a Sunday morning where a more natural and enjoyable experience awaited me on the golf course. Other than those small points we didn't have time for church and we didn't have any relationship with Jesus Christ. We attended church for baptisms, weddings, and funerals. For all intents and purposes we had "played the game" when we got married. We attended church for six months before our wedding date so that the pastor/minister/priest would marry us and then once the official ceremony had been done we stopped going. We didn't feel like we were missing out on something by not going to church because the reality was that we truly did feel that church was a waste of time and had no application to our lives. It also didn't fit into the search for the dream, so Deb threw the invitation in the garbage.

The very next night we were going through the mail again and Deb noticed another invitation from this church. Now, as it turned out the church did not send two separate mailings of invitations. They only sent out one mass mailing to the homes in our area, but by coincidence ... nudge, nudge ... like God orchestrating something to get our attention, we received two invitations to go to this new church. Deb commented that perhaps we should pay attention to this and check this church out. While I didn't verbalize it, my immediate response was a very painful and annoyed "You want me to ... *what*?"

As we walked into the gymnasium, Deb pointed to the very front row and said "come on let's go sit up front" to which I verbally responded in even greater groaning than ever before with, "You want me to ... *what*?" followed by, "No ... we're going to sit in the back row," then I proceeded to stake claim to that entire back row. The back row provided the greatest number of escape routes without drawing attention to myself and I needed to keep all my options open for a quick and painless escape. My body language made it very clear to anyone coming into that gym that no one was invited to join us in that back row because clearly the last thing I needed was for someone to come and sit beside me with an ear-to-ear smile totally happy with life and wanting to carry on a conversation something along the lines of, "Hi, my name is Billy Joe. I haven't seen you here before you must be new. What's your name? Where you from? What do you do for a living and when were you saved and how much do you tithe and do you want to help out at a bake sale this Thursday and how you doing?"

For those of you who have ever had this type of experience while attending a church service you know exactly how uncomfortable this makes people feel. I would rather sit in a dentist's chair and have all my filings removed and new ones put in without any freezing than go through something like that.

I wanted to nip that chance right in the bud and since I was really uncomfortable being at this church thing and I couldn't wait to get out. I was going to make sure that I met absolutely no one and talked to even fewer people than no one.

No one sat down immediately beside me. I saw no clear evidence of any hymn board or organ and the only instruments visible were a couple of guitars, a drum set, and a keyboard. Perhaps this would be a different type of church experience. Could it be possible that the music would not be as painful as I remembered? Then the worship team gathered and began to play some catchy music. It was different and new and had a beat that didn't make me want to fall asleep. There were no hymns or organs, just some uplifting and enjoyable praise songs that were nothing compared to any of my past experiences.

Then, this guy got up and spoke about the Bible in a way that made sense and was easy-to-understand. I don't remember what the message was about, but I was struck by the fact that he didn't wear a robe and several people in the worship team wore blue jeans. Hidden in the sanctuary of our car, afterward, with the doors locked just in case Billy Joe still wanted to introduce herself to me, I felt a calmness and it raised curiosity as to why I felt better after the service than when I went in. This stirred something in me that would eventually change my whole life.

We attended the following Sunday, and, while I wasn't adamant about sitting in the back row, we were definitely in the back section of seats. Before sitting down, I scanned the room looking to see if the previous Sunday had been a fluke, but much to my surprise there was still no hymn board or organ anywhere in sight and it appeared that the guitars were plugged into amps and ready to rip out a couple of power chords. The worship team stepped up on the stage and played a similar style as the previous week. The format was the same as the previous week. I still wasn't "comfortable," but I was curious as to what was going on here.

As my mind drifted off wondering about any hidden conspiracies or traps and how they were plotting to get money out of me, Deb handed a piece of paper to me and directed me to fill it out. It was a welcome card and everyone had been invited to fill it out so that the church would know who was attending and how it could help people out. I filled in the welcome card without ever putting my name down and for months afterwards when the church circulated the prayer calendar it only listed Deb and our children's names. Inside the deep recesses of my mind I had envisioned that the welcome card would be sent to some telemarketing holy call center somewhere in the Midwest and we would end up getting Billy Joe's cousin, Bobby Sue, and her husband Billy Joe II, phoning us each and every week during dinner time checking in to see how we were doing. At least by not having my name on the card they'd always ask for Deb and she'd have to take the survey while the kids and I could continue to eat our dinner and hers would go cold. I didn't want them to know anything about me. But God had other plans and he was using this little church to till the hardened soil of my heart.[5]

---

[5] Proverbs 20:24 "A man's steps are directed by the LORD. How then can anyone understand his own way?" (NIV)

We attended the church a few more times over the winter, and by springtime Deb was attending this church on a regular basis and as she met people, taught in the kids' programs and became more involved, God called her and invited her into many different faith moments. Her faith in and relationship with Jesus Christ started to grow. While she and the kids went to church, I found my religious "experience" on the golf course comprised of eighteen small sermons, if you will, all of them different religious experiences carefully mapped out over some well-manicured grassy areas, followed by a nineteenth experience in the clubhouse afterward. My passion for the game of golf had never changed, neither had my desire to achieve my dream. Our life was comfortable, safe, secure, and on target toward achieving the dream, and even though Deb was developing a deep relationship with Jesus Christ, I totally supported her on her journey so long as it had no impact on me or stopped me from accomplishing my goal of achieving the dream.[6] While I still hadn't achieved what I was looking for to fill the void, I was never more determined to achieve the dream.

As Deb's faith grew stronger, so did her desire to see my heart softened towards God. Her consistent prayer to God was for him to "touch my husband's heart." Nothing more, nothing less, nothing more complicated and nothing simpler than just a prayer made in faith and from her heart.[7] Little did Deb know that God would not only answer the prayer,

---

[6]   Proverbs 19:21 "Many are the plans in a man's heart, but it is the Lᴏʀᴅ's purpose that prevails" (NIV)

[7]   James 5:16 "When a believing person prays, great things happen." (NCV)

but do so in a way that she would never have expected. And it all started with her.

In the fall of that year, she received an invitation to attend the celebration dinner for a recently concluded Alpha program at the church. Alpha is a ten-week program that introduces people to the Christian faith. At the end of every program there's a celebration dinner for the people who have just finished the course and anyone interested in attending the next one. It's kind of like a snapshot introduction to what Alpha is all about, and then during the evening a formal invitation is made for those who want to continue on the following week. Deb invited one of our neighbors to go with her to this celebration evening and on their way home they both decided that they would invite their husbands to go along to the next one.

So, upon her return from the celebration evening, Deb explained to me what Alpha was all about and my radar went up—like spidey-senses—and I knew something was up. I was extremely reluctant to respond to her invitation in any manner that gave any type of inkling that I would consider going so I responded with something that would let her know that I was totally against it. "You want me to ... *what?*" But she was relentless in lobbying my attention to the invitation. Simultaneously, the neighbor was doing the exact same thing with her husband. It wasn't long before he and I met outside our houses, safe from any type of covert interference from our wives and asked each other, "Are you being asked to go to this Alpha thing?"

We realized very quickly the conspiracy going on between our wives. So, in our best efforts to protect our integrity, manliness, and freedom from any further commitments to this whole church thing, we developed a very well thought out counter-conspiracy, anti-viral, firewall protectionist rebuttal. We agreed to attend just once so that our wives would stop hounding us and we further agreed that regardless of what happened during that one-time attendance we would come out of that evening saying to our wives, "You know, honey, we did attend one, but it's not really for me. But you keep going ... good for you and I'll cheer you on." We felt very confident that our plan would work perfectly.

At the first evening upon entering the hall, we were met by people who were really nice. Too nice. My radar was up, my spidey-senses were still tingling, and just as I panned the room and memorized the location of the emergency exits, we were invited to help ourselves to dinner and then watch a video of some guy speaking about the initial elements of Christianity. After the dinner/video the whole group broke into smaller groups to discuss the video in greater detail. I know what you're thinking, right now, and the answer is, yes. My greatest fear had happened. I got put into a group separate from Deb and our neighbors. Their group laughed and joked and appeared to be having a good time. Me, I was completely alone sitting in a circle of fear.

Panic set in, as the leader of my group asked people to introduce themselves. I wait for someone in my group to pipe up and say, "Hi ... my name is Billy Joe ..." Needless to say, I didn't say a single word at all. I sat with my arms crossed in front of my chest and my body language made a very clear statement: "Don't you dare ask me any questions. I'm just watching the clock waiting for the evening to finish so that I can just get in the car, go home and tell my wife that I tried it, but it didn't work out for me ... yadda, yadda, yadda."

The evening took forever, but eventually finished. On the car ride home everyone busily chattered about how enjoyable the different elements of the evening were, everyone except for me. It was all I could do to just get home. I never thought I'd get there when my good buddy said, "This was a good evening, I think I'll be back next week." It was everything I could do to control my reflexes from smacking him upside the head and reminding him of our deal, but all I could think of was the need to scream, "You traitor!" Clearly his agenda was to gain as many brownie points as he possibly could with his wife, and I had no interest in getting more brownie points. All eyes were on me as they realized they had succeeded in separating and dividing us. Now that one of us had given in and gone over to the other side, my mind raced to try and figure how I could keep harmony in my marriage while figuring out what to do.

Think ... think ... think ... There was one positive thing about the evening ... the food. And, if there was any motivation to get me to attend the next week, it would not be as a result of the company, but rather the desire to see what was for dinner. Little did I know that God would use that one element to keep my attention for the remaining nine weeks.

I attended each meeting with the expressed purpose of seeing what was on the menu even though the pattern repeated itself every time—eat, sit around, laugh and joke, watch a video, then break into small groups. While everyone else had started warming up to each other, my only input remained critical and dead set on expressing reasons for why the stuff we were hearing wasn't necessarily true or applicable to my life. On the drive home everyone would comment on how much fun they had and I would ask them what planet they were from and then wonder what would be for dinner the next week. They say the definition of insanity is to continually repeat the same event(s) while expecting a different outcome. That would pretty much summarize the early part of my Alpha experience until one night the stakes got higher and the heat was definitely turned up!

At the conclusion of one our Alpha meetings the leaders were trying to coordinate a place to host the Holy Spirit weekend which is part of the Alpha program. Option after option was being talked about with no successful conclusion as to a location that could host this weekend—that was until Deb offered, out loud, I might add, that she and I would be happy to host the Holy Spirit weekend at our house. It was out of her mouth before I had any involvement in the invitation to participate in the decision. In fact, I had no idea what this weekend was all about because when the larger group was talking about the details of this weekend my mind was wandering and wondering what next week's dinner would be. I knew nothing about the details except to say that by the time I clued in as to what was happening it had gained huge momentum of its own. I had gathered very quickly that this was going to be a really intense weekend since they were trying to do it in one day instead the normal two and a half days. Suddenly my anticipation of next week's meal changed to focus on how very upset my stomach had become and I had a strong desire to get rid of this week's meal ... right then.

The itinerary for that particular day meant that it would be a very long, jammed-packed day. It would start around 8:00 a.m. and go until 10:30 p.m., and all I could think of was having to spend an entire day with a bunch of these whackos from church and then having to go out and see my neighbors on the street the next day and have to explain about this church thing going on at our house that Deb had roped me into. I was not a happy camper with this scenario and my response inside of my head was, "You've got to be kidding"—"You want me to ... *what?*"—but the idea had caught momentum of its own and I just sat there watching as everyone started to plan what was going to go on at our house and I was becoming sick to my stomach.

As the day approached, my anxiety level reached an all-time new peak. I watched all these cars rolling in with insanely and impossibly happy, cheerful people for such an early hour of the morning. All I wanted to do was crawl back into my bed. The day started and a calmness came over me, and as I spent time with this group of people I started to realize that they weren't that bad. By the end of the evening something had definitely happened in my heart. There was a stirring of my spirit in a way that I had never expected or experienced before.

It had snowed a tremendous amount that day and people had to brush off their cars and let them warm up before leaving. While their cars warmed up, everyone huddled inside to say their official goodbyes. As each person left, the remaining group shrank until there was only one couple remaining. They were the leaders involved in running the Alpha course and as they got their coats on I asked just one question that started a dialogue about Christianity that launched a question-and-answer period for almost two hours. They didn't miss a beat when I asked the question and it was probably on the second question that they walked with me back into our family room.

With every question that was answered I would ask another and this guy sat and talked with me patiently answering each question, never once making me feel like I was dumb, inadequate or not worthy of a response. Each question I put out there was me testing the waters to see if this was safe ground for me to continue the dialogue, while Deb and the man's wife moved into the kitchen. Later on I would find out that they were praying the entire time for the Holy Spirit to move and stir my spirit in a powerful way.

Their car was still running while all this was going on. Never once did he get up and say "hold that thought while I go turn my car off." He knew the significance of this moment and if he had stopped it to go outside, turn the car off and come back, the conversation would have ended. He let his car run for almost two hours while this unreached, skeptical critic responded to the stirring of his own spirit. I had not expected something like this to happen, at all, and I knew that given the responses to my questions that my thoughts about the validity of Christianity had changed and I would need to explore this concept further[8] simply because of where I was

---

8   Proverbs 20:27 "Our inner thoughts are a lamp from the LORD, and they search our hearts." (CEV)

at in my own journey and my willingness to keep looking for what I hadn't found, yet.

If this whole "faith thing" was a potential avenue to consider in my searching, then I had to know whether it was true or false, once and for all. If what I had heard about Christianity over the past few weeks in the Alpha program was, in fact, true, then it had great significance to me and my family. Similarly, if it was false, then I wanted to know so that I didn't spend any more time doing something that wasn't going to get me where I needed to be to find what I was still looking for. One way or another I needed to push into it so I could either discard it and continue searching for meaning and purpose by way of my dream, or embrace it and see what journey and path it would take me on. This was not a path I had planned to go down when I started this quest, but it was clearly a path that needed to be explored, and little did I know what lay ahead.[9]

How about you? Is there something going on in your life, right now, that's stirring your spirit? Are you paying attention to the circumstances around it? If it is happening, right now, know that it's the living God trying to get your attention. He's trying to show you what you've been looking for. If there isn't such a stirring going on, right now, then ask yourself about the last time such a thing happened and review the circumstances around it and how you did or didn't react to it at the time. Ask God to reveal to you what He was trying to show you and teach back then, then listen for the answer.

---

[9]   Proverbs 16:9 "We can make our plans, but the Lord determines our steps." (NLT)

Chapter 5

CHANGE IN PLANS— THE HOLY AUDIBLE

"We gain strength, and courage, and confidence
by each experience in which we really stop to look fear in
the face ... we must do that which we think we cannot."
Eleanor Roosevelt

" ... because of our faith in Him, we dare to have
the boldness (courage and confidence) of free access
(an unreserved approach to God with freedom and
without fear)." Ephesians 3:12 (AMP)

"About this time another large crowd had gathered, and
the people ran out of food again. Jesus called his disciples
and told them, "I feel sorry for these people. They have
been here with me for three days, and they have nothing
left to eat. If I send them home hungry, they will faint along
the way. For some of them have come a long distance.
His disciples replied, "How are we supposed to find enough
food to feed them out here in the wilderness?" Jesus asked,
"How much bread do you have?" "Seven loaves," they
replied. *So Jesus told all the people to sit down on the
ground. Then he took the seven loaves, thanked God for
them, and broke them into pieces. He gave them to his
disciples, who distributed the bread to the crowd. A few
small fish were found, too, so Jesus also blessed these and
told the disciples to distribute them.* They ate as much as
they wanted. Afterward, the disciples picked up seven large
baskets of leftover food. There were about 4,000 people in
the crowd that day, and Jesus sent them home after they
had eaten." Mark 8:1–9 (NLT)

Jesus, the disciples and four thousand people had congregated in this deserted, isolated, rural place for three days. Patterns of ministry established by the existing religious power structure would have scoffed at anyone spending time in such a remote area. The preferred pathway for experiencing the presence of God was to require people to come to the Temple and pay homage to the religious structure where they would then be allowed into the presence of the religious elite. That isn't the pathway that Jesus established in this rural location. In essence, it was believed that nothing of any value would or could happen in a remote rural place. But that didn't stop Jesus from going into new areas, doing things differently and stepping into areas that to some made no sense whatsoever.

I marvel at his willingness, and of the disciples, to step off the normal path and into uncharted territory to spend time with people who didn't fit the standard mold, and then set up a camp and bring all of those people into an experience with the living God. After all, they were meeting in Gentile territory, a place normally very hostile toward any gathering of or use by Jews, let alone someone who was publicly calling himself the Messiah to the Jewish nation. But that didn't stop Jesus and he taught his disciples about the shortcomings of following human logic.

This gathering was full of different life stories. Each family with their own story took their spot in the rural isolated field, where logic said nothing of any importance would, should or could happen there. Perhaps some brought their sick friends hoping that Jesus would heal them while others came to be released from spiritual bondage. Still others joined in not because they had any desire to be healed or welcomed into a new community, they wanted in because they believed that they were witnessing something unique and didn't want to miss out on the happening. That's why everyone stayed for three days. It's not like they packed an overnight bag with shaving cream, razors, hair brush, toothbrush, etc., totally prepared for a three day sleepover. Not at all. They wanted to witness something so awesome that they stayed so they wouldn't miss a single thing ... history in the making. And something did happen.

Jesus knew there was this pent-up demand for people to come into an experience with God, to be healed, reconciled, loved (perhaps for the very first time) and to be given validation of their worthiness as a person and accepted for who they were. He knew—and they knew—to be shown all of these things firsthand would make them feel complete, not only in their individual lives, but in the greater community, as well. Things haven't changed much in the last two thousand years.

This Woodstock-type gathering took on a movement all its own, and after three days everyone was tired and hungry. The people looked to the disciples to do something and the disciples became overwhelmed. They had been doing their absolute best to keep things in order, trying to make everyone—regardless of their social or religious status or beliefs—feel welcome. They were exhausted, too, but they knew they were participating in the Kingdom of God moving right before their very eyes. The reality of our humanness meant that at the end of three days of serving, the disciples' patience had run out and their nerves beyond frayed. Perhaps they were grumbling under their breath that it was time for these folks to go on their way.

Yet despite whatever protocol and established rules of etiquette would say, Jesus knew they were tired and so he called them in and instructed his disciples to gather around in a circle. The group gathered in a holy huddle with the disciples probably expecting Jesus to send all the people home. Human logic told them that this was why they were being called to gather. Then Jesus looked at every one of them in the huddle, eye to eye like a quarterback looking at each one of his teammates on the fourth down, one yard to go and victory was in the bag. Instead of Jesus taking a knee and calling it a wrap, he threw a change of plans just before the snap of the ball and calls an audible! Audibles have a way of putting an "!" on something extraordinary. That's what Jesus did here. Jesus called an audible and basically told his disciples that he wanted to do something special to keep their tanks full of enthusiasm and energy for the long journey back to their routine of comfort. So special that every single one of the thousands who had gathered would talk about the experience for years to come with their kids and grandkids.

Audibles happen when God's Spirit wants to move in a zig when the world says it should be a zag. Audibles happen when our burden for humanity meets God's desire to shower us with His presence. It was out of his burden for taking care of the people that Jesus told his inner circle that they should do something that that they wouldn't ever forget and that completely defied logic. What would your response have been?

Jesus locked eyes and told his disciples that they were

actually going to feed these people. In complete unison the disciples responded with, "You want us to ... *what?*"

Meanwhile at that same moment somewhere in the crowd, away from the holy huddle, a family sat, watching everything going on around them. Maybe the husband had been coerced by his wife to check out what was happening and so, just to please her this one time, he agreed to go along with her and the kids. With great expectation that something different was going to happen here, the lady sat, hoped, prayed, and watched for any sign that anything extraordinary was going to happen to her and her family. Perhaps she thought this would be the start of finding a place where the entire family could get to know this Jesus and all of his disciples. A place where they would be invited to join the larger family, a place where they would feel completely welcomed, loved for who they are and a place that they could finally call home. She silently prayed that this be the place where God would reach her husband's heart and so she sat with great hope, watching all of the movement going on in the middle of this rural field.

The husband watched all the goings-on through a skeptic filter and while he watched those so-called "Jesus people" to see if their actions matched their words, he noticed that they seem to have something he knows he doesn't. There was something about these people that didn't fit with how they should be acting, at least according to his previous experiences with these types. It's almost like they're too nice, too welcoming, too accommodating ... just ... too much. This can't be real, but this turned out to be bonus family time and a deep peace has fallen over his family. The kids aren't fussy or complaining, and it's almost as if they know that this is where they're supposed to be.[1]

He watched the disciples break away from Jesus and start handing out food to the people sitting closest to Jesus. He thanked his "lucky stars" that they managed to get a spot so close simply because there's no way that they'd have enough food to get all the way to the back. But, as he watched more closely, he noticed that the food isn't running out. As his family and those around him notice the same thing, a long ripple of awe and praise rushes through the crowd as people realize what they're witnessing ... the unexpected moment where the impossible turns to possible ... and in that moment they experience the loving power of God. It will change their lives, forever.

Oftentimes, God calls us in ways that we would never expect and to do things that make absolutely no sense. Holy audibles defy human logic. These right here ... right now moments have true life changing impact not only for the individual(s) who respond in those moments, but also on the people observing such moments when they happen.

I was that guy sitting and observing something special happening at a rural church, and by the fall after my Alpha experience, once my golf season ended, my Sundays allowed me to spend some time attending Trinity Community Presbyterian Church. This church was formed by the amalgamation of three small rural congregations who had heard God's call to step

---

[1]   Mark 10:14–15 "children are at the very center of life in the kingdom. Mark this: Unless you accept God's kingdom in the simplicity of a child, you'll never get in." *The Message.*

out of their comfort zone and risk doing something really big. They sold their old buildings and collectively decided that if they were going to be a church that impacted their community they were going to have to do something really different than what they had done in the past. They changed how they did church and it was a radical change. It wasn't easy, but those who stayed the course and answered God's audible to become part of something extraordinary were greatly rewarded as they saw people coming to a relationship with Jesus Christ.

The church started out meeting in the gymnasium of a rural elementary school, and before long there was a growing crowd gathering each Sunday. Every week new people joined alongside those who were growing in a relationship with Jesus Christ. People's social and religious status didn't matter. Everyone was welcome and those serving every Sunday just wanted to share that experience with as many people as possible. Word spread that something was going on and people started to check out what was happening in this rural field. Ironically enough, Trinity was meeting in the middle of a rural area where logic and expertise said it would be impossible to keep a church viable. Yet each and every Sunday people gathered to be a part of something special. They gathered to be in the midst of the presence of Jesus Christ. Regardless of who you were or what your background was, you were made to feel welcome. The more I watched the participants and leaders in this congregation the more their words and actions truly reflected what they preached.

After months of observing from the sidelines I started to step out a little and get to know some of the people within this community. When Deb and I finished the Alpha program, God orchestrated something amazing. He created the opportunity for us to experience our very first small group. It's not like this group officially happened nor was it planned by any of us, but as I look back on how it all came together, I realize that God had orchestrated and called this group for a very specific reason and season.

Our get-togethers allowed Deb and me to experience community at a level we had never ever experienced before. I was allowed to feel like I truly belonged even before I believed, and it became even more obvious to me after every get-together with this group that there had to have been a greater power who had removed all the "coincidences" and called together four couples for something very special. Our get-togethers not only allowed me to continue to ask questions about Christianity, but to also see and experience firsthand something very special—biblical community like that in the early church. Like the people in the crowd who had gathered to be in the midst of Jesus Christ, waiting for something special to happen, it seemed every time our group got together we did in fact gather in the midst of Jesus and more often than not something special happened.

During this season I had not lost focus on securing my dream, the golf course, nor had I lost focus on the journey of finding truth, meaning and purpose by way of filling the void of emptiness I so desperately wanted to get rid of. At that moment in time my spiritual efforts stayed focused on continuing to explore the validity and truth of Christianity while my worldly efforts were spent growing my consulting business and working towards building my dream. Deb and I had formed a partnership with another couple and we had secured land to begin building the golf course. My consulting business was growing and business opportunities were opening up on a regular basis which meant that I was spending a good portion of time on the road.

On one of these business trips I found myself traveling through northern Michigan on my way to meet a new client in an area I had never been before. It was a rather long trip by car and so, to fill the time, I had purchased a couple of books to listen to. The first was John Ortberg's *If You Want to Walk on Water, You've Got to Get Out of the Boat* and two other books by Lee Strobel entitled, *The Case For Christ* and *The Case For Faith*. I had been reading these books at home, but the thought of having totally uninterrupted time in the car during this trip to just listen and absorb the points of these books would be valuable in my continued exploration of Christianity.

As I listened to *The Case For Faith*, the author, Lee Strobel, raised many different points of objection with Christianity that he had explored in his own journey and I found myself speaking out loud to the tape player in my car thinking that if I shared my thoughts out loud then Lee Strobel would be able to hear me. Eventually, he would address some of my key objections, but nonetheless, I enjoyed the one-sided banter as I drove down the highway. The insignificant hours flew by and the banter continued until I heard it—a voice coming from within the car that answered each of my objections. It was like someone was sitting in the car with me as I countered every point in favor of Christianity out loud.

I had never heard it before or maybe it had been speaking to me for many years, but the busyness of my life had blocked my ears from hearing it. Or, maybe I had ignored it and adjusted my own volume level to it so that I could lie to myself and plead ignorance to its call. Or, perhaps my life had been too cluttered with my own selfish desires and I was too busy working on my to-do list that I didn't explore or answer the voice further. Nonetheless, on that evening of October 24, I started to get a little uncomfortable as I looked around the car trying to locate this voice. The quicker I responded to the voice with my own objections to the points it raised, the faster and stronger the counterpoints were raised to counter my objections—this wrestling continued for quite some time. I was so occupied with what was going on that I hadn't noticed the sun had set long ago and the blackness of the night had engulfed everything around me.

God calls to us in our mundane, insignificant day-to-day routines and He does it in ways that we would never expect; inspired audibles that challenge our human logic. Have you had those moments where perhaps you've heard that voice, but you've tuned it out or ignored it because you've been too busy working on the to-do list or the task at hand? Maybe there have been moments in your life when you've felt the prompting to go left instead of right even though your head said go right, and you were met by a small unexpected blessing that would never have occurred if you had followed your own path. God calls to us in ways that are always unique, rarely repeated, but oftentimes blocked out by our day-to-day routines and so we may miss the invitation to step into an experience of standing in His midst, and we miss the unexpected surprise of a burning bush as told in the story of Moses.

There was nothing special about this particular day in Moses' life. He was tending the flock of his father-in-law leading them far into the wilderness, far away from the comforts of home when God stepped into the mundane routine of daily life in a small, but unique way. He invited Moses into His midst.[2] Moses wasn't expecting an experience in the midst of his shepherding, but was prompted to take a different path—to go left instead of right—a path he'd never gone on before to a place he'd never been to before to an area he'd didn't really know that well. God used a small burning bush to get his attention from the mundane routine of comfort.

God does this all the time. He tries to catch our attention, but we miss these moments because of our preoccupation with completing the task at hand, and the day-to-day routines of our lives numb us from being open to and seeing God moving all around us in unexpected ways.

When Moses saw the burning bush, he didn't freak out or runaway or cry for help. Instead, his first reaction was to acknowledge how unique and amazing this was. Then, his curiosity led him to wander closer to the bush to try to figure out why the bush was not being consumed by the flames.[3] Is that our typical reaction to unexpected, amazing and impossible things we see or experience along the way? God used something small and insignificant (a small bush) to first get Moses' attention and

---

[2] See Exodus 3:1–10

[3] Exodus 3:2–3 "Moses stared in amazement. Though the bush was engulfed in flames, it didn't burn up. "This is amazing," Moses said to himself "Why isn't this bush burning up? I must go see it" (NLT)

to see how receptive and aware he was to His presence. How many little moments like that have we all missed?

Was my hearing this voice in the car like that of Moses' seeing the burning bush? In my own mind, the tapes I was listening to were in fact small and insignificant, and I had no idea what was going to happen when I put the first tape into the machine. However, as the hours passed and I started to debate with the points raised on those tapes, God stepped into what had started out as a normal and ordinary moment and quickly turned it into an unexpected and extraordinary event. For each and every point/reason I raised for not following Jesus Christ, this voice countered. For someone who had a strong and very successful sales background, the constant countering wasn't hard to take. What made it difficult was that I wasn't used to being out counter-countered in such a strong and effective way. I was used to being able to counter someone else's objection as to why they shouldn't buy into something and then convince them to change their mind. But, in this moment in my car, I was not prepared for the other side to have such a strong counter-counter argument. The whole thing went on for some time and then I was hit with the final point, one that drew me to the threshold of something truly significant.

The voice said, "Why are you running? Why are you afraid? Come to me."

My immediate response was, "You want me to ... *what? Right here? Right now?*"[4]

For the first time in my life, I truly understood what Jesus had

---

[4]   Revelation 3:20 "Here I am! I stand at the door and knock. If anyone hears my voice and opens the door, I will come in ... " (NIV)

done for me and that all of my objections to Christianity were, in fact, based on fear. At the end of the day, I was afraid that if I committed my life to following Jesus Christ, I would lose all my options and escape plans. I will never forget the significance of that moment as long as I live. I stood at the threshold where fear and faith collide, and I knew that this moment was no ordinary happening, but one that had very important consequences based on my response. How about you?

Audibles take us to the threshold, the place where we meet Jesus Christ, and it's in the collision between fear and faith where extraordinary personal moments of transformation occur. They're right here ... right now moments. I felt that this moment was significant and had eternal consequences, and it wasn't long before the enemy was there with the suggestion that said, "Oh, just dismiss it because this isn't really happening," and, yet, I felt that if I didn't deal with this moment it might never happen again. And so, with tears flowing from my eyes, I listed everything that I had done in my life that I knew wasn't right, including certain aspects of my lifestyle, and I stepped through the threshold of forgiveness, I stepped from fear into faith and placed my life at His feet asking for forgiveness of my past and giving my future to His way for me. I stepped through that threshold, hoping for forgiveness and cleansing from all of my past and emerged on the other side certain of His promise to free and cleanse me from my past.[5] I can't explain the peace that flooded over me except to say that I knew that I was in the midst of Jesus Christ and that things

---

[5] 1 John 1:9 "If we confess our sins, he is faithful and just and will forgive us our sins and purify us from all unrighteousness" (NIV)

were never going to be the same.

Now, I know that God has a sense of humor because this event occurred on October 24 at 9:15 p.m. and I hadn't noticed any other cars on the road for quite some time. In fact, it was getting to that point in my journey where I was starting to get uncomfortable as I had drifted into the wilderness of northern Michigan not really sure of where I was, nor did I have a clear understanding of where I needed to be or how I was going to get there. I was alone on the road and it seemed like the thickness of the night swallowed the light from my headlights. There was no one else around at least until 9:30 p.m. when I noticed a flashing blue light fast approaching in my rearview mirror. I'm sure Jesus had a little smile on his face since the only cars having flashing blue lights in Michigan were state troopers and he was in hot pursuit of someone. It didn't take long for me to realize that the someone he was after was me! God was giving me a little laugh just to lighten what had been the most intense emotional period of my spiritual life.

As I pulled over to the side of the road the trooper followed me, and when I put my car in park the trooper turned on a spotlight from his car that was so powerful it lit up not only everything in my car but also the road ahead for many miles. It reminded me of the scene in National Lampoon's Christmas Vacation when Chevy Chase finally gets all of the Christmas outdoor lights on his house (thousands of them) to turn on.

As he approached the car, I rolled down the window, trying to seem totally composed and together, while he asked me if I knew how fast I was going. I'm sure he was looking at me and starting to question my abilities to drive a car as he took one glance at me. I was an emotional wreck and I must've looked like something really special after having just had quite an emotional experience with the living God. Anyway, I answered that I had no idea how fast I had been traveling as I had been a little sidetracked over the last several miles. Without exploring that response any further he asked for my driver's license, ownership, and insurance, and, upon receipt, returned to his car to write up the ticket or to quite possibly check with his buddies to see if they, too, had ever run into Canadians who looked and acted a little weird. As I waited for the trooper to return, I couldn't help but laugh when I noticed that the spotlight from the state trooper's car lit up the road for miles and as I looked down the road an exit sign off in the distance glowed in the light.[6] When the trooper handed me my ticket, driver's license, and information, I got back on the road, trusting that God would get me to my destination. That exit sign was the one I needed to take to continue my journey[7] into uncharted territory.

Reflecting on the significance of that moment, I can't help but wonder how many other times Jesus stood knocking at the doorway of my life calling and waiting for me to open the door, to meet him at the threshold of my life. Thresholds are transitional doorways in our lives that awaken our spirit and take us from the known areas of comfort into new unknown

---

[6] Psalm 18:28 "Suddenly, God, you floodlight my life" *The Message*

[7] Proverbs 3:6 "Seek his will in all you do, and he will show you which path to take" (NLT)

territories of learning about ourselves. They separate those old and new parts in our lives—feeling unloved to knowing we're loved, rejected to accepted, anxiety to peace, despair to hope, alone to community ... . These moments centering on the doorways of our lives where two opposite forces collide in the midst of the thresholds of our lives are right here ... right now moments. Thresholds are where change occurs and we enter new and uncharted territory.

In the movie, *The Fellowship of the Ring*, part one of the *Lord of the Rings* trilogy, Frodo and Sam set off on an adventure that takes them into the world of the unknown, and as they walk through some fields Sam comes to an abrupt stop while Frodo continues marching on. When he eventually realizes that Sam is no longer with him, Frodo stops and looks back towards Sam and asks why he has stopped.

Sam states, "This is it. If I take one more step it will be the farthest away from home I've ever been," and as he steps over the threshold into uncharted territory, Sam reminds Frodo of the advice they received from Bilbo, Frodo's uncle, who said, "It's a dangerous business going out your door. You step onto the road and if you don't keep your feet there is no knowing where you might be swept off to."[8] As the two characters walk through the field during this dialogue the camera pans back and shows a scarecrow behind them, appearing like the third party in this conversation. Sam has met his fear of going into the unknown and once he's made the decision to continue, to step into the unknown and uncharted new world, the part that is furthest from the safety

---

[8]   *The Lord of the Rings: The Fellowship of the Ring* (Alliance Atlantis, 2001)

of home, the camera changes angles and pulls back even more, and you're left with a truly stunning visual picture of the beautiful valleys and mountains that await Sam and Frodo in their continuing adventure.

The visual imprint of this portion of the film truly defines the threshold between two elements—fear, which holds us back from seeing the broader picture and the beauty that lies ahead if we would but step outside of the known and into the unknown; and, courage to have faith, which is the act of meeting our fear and stepping through the threshold into the unknown adventure that lies ahead. We need courage to discover the attributes of our faith and to live in that faith. This is where collisions of life altering forces take place—the known versus the unknown, fear versus faith, good versus evil and so it is with our own individual lives.

Biblically, doorways and thresholds are "often associated with entrance into areas of great spiritual significance."[9] John Ortberg says, "fear disrupts faith and becomes the biggest obstacle to trusting and obeying God."[10] It's fear that holds us back from a deeper experience with Jesus, but also from finding out who we really are, whose we are, and the wonderful adventure He's calling us to participate in.

We have all had different situations in our lives that have centered on the opening and closing of doors. Do you remember the first time you were alone? Go back into your

---

[9] Leland Ryken, James C. Wilhoit, Tremper Longman III, General Editors, *Dictionary of Biblical Imagery,* (Downer's Grove, IL: IVP Academic a division of InterVarsity Press, 1998), 215.

[10] John Ortberg, *If You Want to Walk on Water, You've Got to Get out of the Boat,* (Grand Rapids, MI: Zondervan Publishing House, 2001), 120.

snapshot of memories to the first time you were left alone in the house, remember? Remember when your parents were walking out the door and they stood on the threshold looking back and giving final instructions not to answer the door because of the potential that a stranger could be the one on the other side. As a result, fear set in and, in fact, stood outside the doorway for the entire evening. When you were finally alone, you did whatever you wanted—play the music really loud and pretend that you're on tour, your best rendition of Tom Cruise in Risky Business; you were free to watch whatever you wanted on TV, and eat whatever you wanted to, wherever you wanted to.

What if the anticipation of that wild and crazy night had been frozen from coming to life because of that one nagging thought in the back of your mind that festered with each passing moment—what if someone knocks on the door? What if that one fear had held us back from doing any of the things we were feeling called to do. Our evening would be ruined because we'd spend the entire time worrying about what would be on the other side of that door if someone knocked. We'd miss the thrill of a new adventure. It would keep us totally paranoid and frozen in fear.

Imagine as this pattern repeats itself time after time until this one time you're alone and there's a knock on the door and fear enters your mind. It plays tricks with you. "Should I answer it or should I sit here totally frozen and not move? Should I, shouldn't I? Should I, shouldn't I?" This mental tennis game goes back and forth until somewhere deep within you strength rises to the surface to take action and actually open the door. You tell yourself, "Enough of this. I'm going to take charge and not sit here frozen in fear, anymore." You get to the door and with every ounce of courage you turn the door handle and open the door to look out on a whole new world. You deal with the person who has knocked on the door—the salesmen, Jehovah's Witness, or the Girl Guide selling cookies. You deal with it. You handle the situation. True to the ingredient of experience, the more times you do something like answering the door when you're alone in the house, the more confident you become that what is on the other side of the door is not a threat and certain that the experience of opening the door will be a positive one.[11]

Once you face the fear of opening the door, the experience of standing at that threshold heightens and builds your level of faith and confidence that things will be just fine if you do in fact open the door. You handle the situation successfully and you go back to your activities with a greater swagger in your step because you've dealt with the old element of fear and experienced a new component of faith. You turn the stereo back on and crank the music a little louder. It's not that the fear of the unknown ever goes away, it's just that the more times we deal with it and stare it in the face, the more it loses its hold over us,[12] the hold that keeps us from stepping through the threshold and experiencing something brand new. We can all remember moments where we have opened the door with great trepidation and have been completely and pleasantly surprised at who/what was standing on the other side.

---

[11] Hebrews 11—definition of faith

[12] Ortberg, *If You Want to Walk on Water,* 22.

A good friend of mine was home alone, one day, when someone knocked at his front door. With great reluctance he opened the door to find a very beautiful woman standing at his doorway who had volunteered to do some enumerating for an upcoming election. One thing led to another and they began a conversation which led to a first date which eventually led to ... you guessed it ... the altar. This would be a great example of opening a door, being pleasantly surprised at what was on the other side and literally stepping over the threshold.

Our first step over the threshold of a right here ... right now moment is one we will always remember, going from the known to the unknown, and regardless of what motivates us to step through, there is always great excitement and adventure that awaits us on the other side. It may not be the adventure we expect or anticipate, but it is guaranteed to take us into the unknown and that's what God has waiting for us—a brand new adventure. What enhances our experience at the threshold of the doorway is, in fact, the realization that fear has anchored itself in an area of our lives, an area where we have given permission for it to establish roots, control, and power in our physical and spiritual lives, and unless we walk across the threshold of faith, that fear will always have power over us. This is not the way God intended our lives to be. He meant for our lives to be "an adventure to be lived. That's the nature of it and has been since the beginning when God set the dangerous stage for this high-stakes drama and called the whole wild enterprise *good*. He rigged the world in such a way that it only works when we embrace *risk* as the theme of our lives, which is to say, only when we live by faith"[13] and only when we answer His call to step through the threshold on a regular basis.

Since the very beginning of time, God has been actively pursuing us and calling us to step across the threshold from fear to liberation, oppression to freedom, ordinary to extraordinary, death to salvation, loneliness to relationship.[14] So, ask yourself at this very moment where is Jesus knocking in your life, right now, and what is the root of the fear that is holding you back from opening the door and stepping towards Him?

Fear holds us back ... faith calls us forward. Fear is the whisper of doubt that attempts to disable our innate ability to trust in the one who created us, the one who has a great purpose for us and who calls us to the extraordinary.[15] What's at stake when we answer God's call is a whole new understanding of ourselves, the world around us, and the invitation to an adventure that we would never have chosen for ourselves had we been left on our own to choose. It's a life filled with audibles and it's the way He designed for us to thrive.

---

[13] John Eldredge, *Wild at Heart,* (Nashville, TN: Thomas Nelson Publishers, 2001), 200.

[14] Genesis 3:8–10

[15] Jeremiah 6:16 "This is what the LORD says: "Stand at the crossroads and look; ask for the ancient paths, ask where the good way is, and walk in it, and you will find rest for your souls." (NIV)

Chapter 6

ENTERING THE ROOM
ON STRAIGHT STREET

"A calling is something you discover, not something
you choose." John Ortberg

"Receive and experience the amazing grace of the
Master, Jesus Christ, deep, deep within yourselves."
Philippians 4:23 (The Message)

My wife and I were attending our son's basketball game
when a friend of ours joined us in the stands. He told us
how they had recently purchased a new computer for his
wife's growing photography business. She had taken a vast
number of pictures and this computer was going to make
a great impact on the business. Despite all of the ads on
television that claimed how easy it was to switch from one
computer to another they had nonetheless spent countless
hours learning how to use the new computer and associated
software. She had just been retained to take another family
portrait over the holidays and this new computer with all
of its new software would make things a lot easier in being
able to edit, package, and present the pictures. In the case
of this one particular family, their pictures were going to be
the test case for the new computer and software, in theory,

of course. The pictures were loaded into the computer and the husband hit the one particular button on the keyboard that would permanently delete all of the pictures. He was holding his composure quite well as he shared this story with us and I must admit that he looked rather calm about the whole thing.

The bad news is that they were unsuccessful in their many attempts to retrieve the pictures, but the good news is they're still married. I don't know where the computer is and to this day the pictures have never been found.

I couldn't help but feel empathy for him, as every one of us have tried to help others out and sometimes our efforts cause things to go astray. My heart ached for them simply because we've all had moments like that. The reality in our world, today, is that computers have become such integral components to our lives that everyone of us can relate to that type of experience. We've all been in a situation where we have had to switch from using a different type of computer, operating system, upgraded operating system or software to another. We struggle through the process of rewiring our brains to think differently, to shift from the established structures of the old to learning the ways of the new. Our very own central processing units (our brains) have to learn new ways of thinking all the time and at a pace that only continues to accelerate. We're bombarded with new and improved things every second of every day. New ideas, new perspectives, new ways of doing things, all in an effort to become better and the process itself of upgrading is very frustrating, painful and full of uncertainty, despite whatever the advertisements promise.

We begin the upgrading process with the end in mind—we'll be able to do things faster, stronger, quicker, yet every single one of us just wants to hit the fast forward button and skip the pain around the process of upgrading and rewiring our way of thinking. The process itself is surrounded by the darkness of the unknown and it's guaranteed that somewhere in the process of upgrading we'll throw our hands up and cry out, "Forget it, I'm going back to the way it was!!!" It happens every time we go through a frustrating period when we have to learn a new way of doing things in our spiritual lives, as well. It's painful, but if we persist through the period of darkness we come out the other side rewired, better, stronger and with a totally new perspective.

The Bible recounts such a story in the Book of Acts—the conversion of Saul.[1]

> "All this time Saul was breathing down the necks of the Master's disciples, out for the kill. He went to the Chief Priest and got arrest warrants to take to the meeting places in Damascus so that if he found anyone there belonging to the Way, whether men or women, he could arrest them and bring them to Jerusalem." (Acts 9:1–2 *The Message*)

Saul was "this fuming, raging, hateful man who wanted to kill every last one of the Lord's disciples."[2] Here was a guy

---

[1] See Acts 9:1–19

2 Chris Seay and Brian MacLaren, *The Dust Off Their Feet,* (Nashville, TN: Thomas Nelson Inc., 2006), 40.

who had a plan, a very strong and detailed mission, a to-do list that left no room for variation or uncertainty in his plans for the day, week, month or years to come. He was someone of significance within the Jewish and Roman community. He had status, pull, resources, and even a group of followers prepared to do anything he asked them to do and in this particular account Saul had a very specific plan for himself and the group. They were to set out and eliminate this new and growing movement known as followers of Jesus, Christians, and to do it in such a way that it would be stopped from ever restarting again. They all knew what the plan was. They knew the how, where, when, why and who of Saul's plan. The plan was well thought out and left no room for any deviation.

This particular day started off just like any other. Saul woke up, had breakfast, got caught up on the local news, checked his mail, walked the dog and then reviewed his to-do list. Saul's eyes go straight to the first item on that list: go to the Chief Priest and pick up the permission slips that would allow him entrance into the synagogues in Damascus. He didn't start his day in prayer asking God what He would like him to do that day. No, he told himself what was to be done that day and set about coordinating his plan to make this happen. Permission slips in hand, he heads off to meet the rest of the group at the predetermined place and time. The group set off on the road to Damascus to fulfill Saul's plan. No one told Saul that there was a strong difference between "our best laid plans," our to-do lists and God's plan for us.

"He set off. When he got to the outskirts of Damascus, he was suddenly dazed by a blinding flash of light. As he fell to the ground, he heard a voice: 'Saul, Saul, why are you out to get me?' He said, 'Who are you, Master?' 'I am Jesus, the One you're hunting down. I want you to get up and enter the city. In the city you'll be told what to do next.'

His companions stood there dumbstruck—they could hear the sound, but couldn't see anyone—while Saul, picking himself up off the ground, found himself stone-blind. They had to take him by the hand and lead him into Damascus. He continued blind for three days. He ate nothing, drank nothing."[3]

Everything in Saul's world changed when Jesus stepped in and alters Saul's to-do list. In fact, Jesus rewired Saul's internal operating system and the whole experience of meeting Jesus Christ brought Saul to his knees, a position completely foreign to this powerful man. His well thought out plans were not that important, anymore. Jesus stepped in to meet Saul face to face. Saul was brought to his knees by a light from heaven so bright it forced him to close his eyes and the whole experience shook Saul to the core of his being. The fear of the unexpected and unknown brought him to his knees—this was Saul's *right here ... right now* moment.

Right here ... right now moments are not Jesus' way of frightening us, but His way of announcing/calling/inviting

---

3   Acts 9: 3–9 *The Message*

us to a new plan of action,[4] and that, like learning how to use new software or operating systems, can be very uncomfortable. These are moments when the living God steps into the routine of our daily lives and interrupts our very own, well thought out plans regardless of where we are or what we're doing, without regard for whether or not this might be a convenient time. Saul's life was good. He had it "going on" so to speak, and he was a somebody with a plan for his life. He had never asked for direction, guidance or input from Jesus about his to-do list. Nonetheless, Jesus stepped into Saul's life, interrupted the flow of things and began to rewire Saul's operating system. God's plan for Saul's life was different than what Saul had carefully crafted out on his own. God had something totally different for him to participate in and for Saul to become aware of God's plan, he had to be interrupted by a right here ... right now moment—the road to Damascus.

Everyone has Damascus Road moments where God steps in to rewire our operating system. That's a given. It's going to happen and not just once. There will be operating updates and security patches that God sends to our operating system throughout our lives, and they always require us to accept or decline the upgrade. Sometimes we say yes and other times we say no, but one thing is for sure: God's desire to fully upgrade our operating system is genuine and motivated out of His love for us and His desire to be in relationship with us. His desire for us to have the best possible life means that

---

4   Robert W. Wall, *The New Interpreters Bible Commentary, Volume X* (Nashville, TN: Abingdon Press, 2002) 150.

despite the many different ways God reaches into your life and mine, He'll do so when it's inconvenient, unexpected, and we'll never see it coming.

Regardless of how frightening and unpredictable these moments are, the important element is our response. Do we accept the upgrade, reboot our system according to God's plan, and then learn how to use the new operating system and software? Or, do we decline the upgrade, hoping that we can put it off another day? How we respond to the invitation to an upgrade affects our ability to produce quality output. How we respond to such upgrades matters.

Saul didn't tell Jesus to leave him alone. He loses all sense of direction not only during the experience on the road, but also for another three days. Everything in his life had changed and what was once north is, in fact, south. What he thought was up is now down and his mission, the to-do list, and all of his priorities in life have shifted.[5] Everything in Saul's life was made new because he was given a totally new perspective on the power of Jesus Christ, and call on his life for him to follow a new direction.

Can you imagine a light so powerful that it brings you to your knees, then once you get up, Jesus tells you to go to a room on Straight Street and everything is totally silent? You now have no authority over the men in your group who have just witnessed something unbelievable happen to you. You've been humbled, totally exposed, and there's nowhere to run because you can't see. You can't pose anymore as there's

---

[5]   Acts 9:15 "Saul is my chosen instrument to take my message to the Gentiles and to kings, as well as to the people of Israel" (NLT)

no room to hide. Whatever mask you've been wearing as a self-imposed, really important person has now been ripped off and all you're trying to do at that very moment is to stand up. You attempt to open your eyes and while you feel your eyelids blinking non-stop you can't see a single thing while your mind continually replays the past few moments.

Suddenly, your brain registers that you really can't see even though your sight was fine moments before. Panic sets in and you call out for your companions to assist you as you try to stand up and steady your feet on the ground. You're trying your very best to gain your composure, to get your bearings, and to do it without totally freaking out and showing people any weakness. After he got to his feet, Saul was lead to a house on Straight Street. Think about this for a moment. He's lead to a house he's never been in before, not to mention that he can't see anything to get his bearings and when he's lead to this house, where everything is strange, he's still trying to figure out at what's just happened. He's in no mood for conversation or company. My guess is that the only place he would want to be lead to once inside the house would be a bedroom where he could try to gather his composure without anyone seeing him struggle to understand what is happening to him. He's lead to a room on Straight Street and his days of posing like someone important are done.

Can you relate to this in your own life? If you were to be brutally honest with yourself—and God—are there areas in your life where you operate like a Saul? If God reached into your life, right now, and He totally turned your world upside down where you had to rely on someone else just to get you on your feet, would you be able to trust them and reach out your hand for help like Saul did? It's not easy asking others, let alone God, for help, or relying on them for the very basic elements of survival, is it?

In a very brief but powerful moment, everything has changed and you need someone else to help you when you've never needed it before. You're forced to completely trust them to direct you to where Jesus has instructed you to be. One step at a time. Leaning on God's guidance through someone else while your senses adjust. It wasn't easy for Saul[6]—it wasn't easy for me—and it won't be easy for you when it happens, but rest assured it will happen. God will want you to meet or get reacquainted with His son, Jesus. He'll stop you in your tracks and direct you to go to the room on Straight Street.[7]

The time we spend in the room on Straight Street has no limits. It's unpredictable, sometimes repetitive, painful and full of learning. God will not abandon us here because this is where we also learn just how far we've strayed from His plans for us. Yet, if we choose to respond to God's direction to go to the room on Straight Street, we will be brought back on mission, His mission for us.[8] It's here that God rewires us. It's

---

[6] Jeremiah 10:23 "O Lord [pleads Jeremiah in the name of the people], I know that [the determination of] the way of a man is not in himself; it is not in man [even in a strong man or in a man at his best] to direct his [own] steps." (AMP)

[7] Deuteronomy 4:30–31 "When you are in distress and all these things have happened to you, then in later days you will return to the Lord your God and obey him. For the Lord your God is a merciful God; he will not abandon or destroy you ... " (NIV)

[8] Jeremiah 29:11 "For I know the plans I have for you," says the Lord. "They are plans for good and not for disaster, to give you a future and a hope." (NLT)

never easy and we do not know how long we'll be there, but one thing is for sure—God uses our pain to get our attention.

C.S. Lewis stated that "pain insists upon being attended to. God whispers to us in our pleasures, speaks to us in our conscience, but shouts in our pain. It is His megaphone to rouse a deaf world."[9] Straight Street moments involve the rewiring process of our internal processing unit. Saul's hard drive was being completely redone and updated with a new operating system, new software, and the absolutely best anti-virus program on the market. All of the emotions that Saul was experiencing at that very moment would have been completely contrary and opposite to what his own personal strengths would have wanted to control. He was completely vulnerable, and this would have been very foreign to him and to those around him who were observing all of the happenings. To make things even more interesting, he's led to a house on Straight Street in the city of Damascus where for three days he's blind and has nothing to eat or drink. The only thing he's able to do is pray, listen for God to speak and to submit to the call of God. It must have been the longest three days in Saul's life.[10]

We experience that every time we install an update to a computer. You are notified of the update, you start the process of downloading the update, begin the installation then wait. Wait for the prompt of whether or not the update was successful. If it was, then you're told to restart the computer so that the updates can take effect. Saul was doing the same thing.

---

[9] Owen Collins, *To Quote C.S. Lewis,* (Great Britain: Harper Collins Publishers, 2000), 75.

[10] Psalm 27:14 "Wait patiently for the LORD. Be brave and courageous. Yes, wait patiently for the LORD." (NLT)

Time spent in the room on Straight Street is filled with quiet, lonely moments where we're completely vulnerable to the movement of the Holy Spirit. Being vulnerable is hard for any of us to embrace. Waiting is even harder as the world continues to tell us that we need to have every moment of our days completely filled with things to do, and that we need to do those things as fast as we can so that we can accomplish even more, and if we can continually multi-task while we're filling those precious never-to-return moments of time then we'll be viewed as strong and really important. We're led to believe that whatever we have to sacrifice to fill that moment will be worth it.

We don't like waiting let alone waiting on someone else. It makes us feel vulnerable, weak and unproductive or so the world tells us. Yet the Bible says that it's in our weakness that God gives us strength.[11] Regardless of how long it takes for us to receive these upgrades—three days, three months, or three years—they're necessary for us to become stronger in our relationship with God and those around us. It's on the other side of the pain that we experience in these rewiring moments that we find God's mission and new direction for our lives. As we finish the story of Saul, we see that Saul saw things totally differently following this experience, and his priorities were radically changed. The very foundation of his priorities was recast and reset, and Saul never saw it coming. And neither do we.

I never saw it coming in my own journey, either. Except

---

[11] See Psalm 136:23, Romans 8:26, 1 Corinthians 1:25, 2 Corinthians 12:9, Hebrews 11:34

my mission wasn't to destroy Christians, it was to build my dream, and, since accepting Jesus Christ as my Lord and Savior, things had been moving along just fine. I was now on the winning team and it was fine with me if everything was going to stay just the way it was. Our family had become more involved in our church community, Deb was teaching in the kids' ministry on a regular basis, and I had begun to participate on the worship team. In addition, I was given the invitation to share a very short testimony during a Christmas Eve service which eventually led to other opportunities to speak from the platform. After each speaking opportunity, some people kindly suggested that I should go into the Ministry. I wasn't sure which ministry they were referring to—Ministry of Defense, Tourism, Environment, New Computer Updates—until they said very specifically that I should become a minister. I envisioned myself as a guy dressed in a robe with a collar all the while smiling at them and thinking to myself ... "You want me to ... *what?*"

On the business side, things were moving according to my plan, my own Road to Damascus, if you will. We were working toward securing the rezoning of the land to start building the golf course. My mission had become very clear. I was called to be the best husband, father, and Christian that I possibly could while making my dream a reality. I was focused, on a mission, and the top priority on my to-do list was to get that golf course built. What I didn't anticipate was spending time in the room on Straight Street. I just thought that once I walked through the threshold of the doorway to accepting Jesus Christ as my Lord and Savior, that nothing would affect the status quo of my plan. Funny thing about God, His plan and perspective is not like ours.[12]

We had, along with our partners, purchased the most spectacular piece of land on which to build the golf course. The land wasn't on the market, but with a little hard work I was able to secure it. Its topography was second to none. In fact, from the crest of the highest point on the property you could see westerly at least fifty kilometers/ thirty miles, and many times I would watch the sun set in the distance over the escarpment near Georgian Bay. The entire sky would turn pink, red, and yellow. It was truly the brush of God painting a picture that only He could do. Upon this crest was a tree where I would often spend quiet time sitting there looking at the beauty that God had made and thanking Him for it while painting in my mind what my dream would look like when the golf course was built. It was my favorite spot on the land and we'd just hang out together, me and God. It was peaceful and calming. They were truly wonderful Holy Spirit-filled moments whenever I was there, and I'd always feel closer to God after time spent at this spot.

It was during one of those moments when I heard the voice speak. It was the same voice I'd heard during my trip to northern Michigan. While I was walking near the tree, the voice said, "Sell it." I wasn't expecting to hear, "Sell it." I should've realized that it would have been a very good time for me to put both fingers in my ears and scream, "la la la

---

[12] Isaiah 55:8–9 "I don't think the way you think. The way you work isn't the way I work." God's Decree. "For as the sky soars high above earth, so the way I work surpasses the way you work, and the way I think is beyond the way you think.." *The Message.*

la la ... I'm not listening," but I didn't. My response was, "Sell what? The car, the dog, the house, what? The voice responded after a while with, "Sell the dream." There was a swelling of a tidal wave in my stomach and I thought I was going to be sick right there by the tree and it was very similar to that moment after the check. I didn't even get to, "You want me to ... *what*?"

I answered, in no uncertain terms, "No. There is no way that I'm selling MY dream!!! Come on. Go tell somebody else to sell their dream. It's not fair. It's mine and I worked hard to get to this point. I'm not hurting anyone. I promise to give my tithe to the church and give back to the community and I promise to be nice, to do my chores, to even clean up my room, but there is no way I'm going to sell the golf course."

I was not happy and I left that spot by the tree in quite a huff.

It wasn't long before I was back on the land and sitting near the tree. During my time away, I had been trying to discern what God was up to and whether or not He had misdialed or made a mistake the last time He called me. As I approached the tree, I cried out to Him that it made no sense for me to sell the golf course. I pleaded the lack of fairness in His call and stated that it really wasn't necessary. As I got quiet and looked out on the majestic view over the valley before me, the valley that He had created, I asked if He remembered our last conversation and if He'd had a chance to think about the points I had raised for Him the last time and whether or not He'd reconsidered. There was nothing but silence then after a while, God spoke and said, "Sell the golf course and go back to school to get your Master of Divinity."

"School? You've got to be kidding! There is NO WAY I'm going back to school!" Case closed. I reflected on the last time I had even mentioned going back to school in any way. I had been invited to attend an awards ceremony put on by the National Post newspaper and the Schulich School of Business at York University in Toronto. It was put on for students who had graduated with their MBA and I had been invited to attend this ceremony by one of my previous trainees from the days when I worked in the real estate company. He had decided to go back to school and get this MBA degree and not only had he graduated from the program, but upon graduation he had been selected to receive an award as the most promising graduate in his class. It was a big deal and he had invited a few of us to see him receive the award and help him celebrate.

I remember being struck by the majority of winners who upon accepting their awards would stand up and tell everyone how much they had already accomplished in their lives by rhyming off a list of well-versed "look at what I've done" accomplishments. Each trying to out do the other. It made for a very long evening for those of us in the audience. However, what really struck me was how no one gave thanks to God in any of their speeches and this realization made me sit up and look at things through different eyes. No one acknowledged God, not even to say grace before dinner. God was showing me my past circle and I was acutely aware of how my spiritual journey to Straight Street had changed my perspective. At the conclusion of the evening I was walking out of the building with a good friend of mine and he asked me if that ceremony made me want to go back to school to get my master's degree. I responded, "I will never go back to school, especially for a master's degree of any kind." The old saying "never say never" is so true!

So, after hearing God call me to sell the dream and go back to school, it didn't take long for me to step right back into and continue my lobbying efforts from our last visit. My rant went something like this, "You know, I didn't sign up for this part. It's not like the Kingdom will suffer or miss out if I sit this one out. May I remind you that I'm not really scholastically inclined, remember? You made me that way and besides, seriously, I'm not equipped to do that. You've gifted me in other areas and I'm better at the whole business/ golf combination. You know, God, I can use the golf course to reach people here in the community and make a greater impact than any other business in the area." The rant went on for sometime and I was quite proud of the list of counterpoints raised and how I'd rhymed them off so quickly feeling like God would be impressed. However, after a short period when there was no response at all, just the wind blowing the leaves of the tree, I started to feel nervous like I had offended God in some small way. That was not my intent, but the silence was getting to me. I wonder if that's what Saul felt during his three days of silence in that room on Straight Street.

Silence can make us feel uncomfortable, can't it? Elisabeth Kubler-Ross says these types of moments are gifts for us to "learn to get in touch with the silence within yourself, and know that everything in life has purpose. There are no mistakes, no coincidences, all events are blessings given to us to learn from." These are moments in the room on Straight Street, filled with great opportunities for our souls to be fed, and, if we're to learn about ourselves and what God has in store for us, then we must silence the daily distractions of our lives and listen for God to speak. The life of our souls is at stake.[13]

So, as the silence built to where I thought perhaps I had out-trumped God with my clever rebuttals, He finally spoke and said, "I don't need another golf course to be built in the world, but I do need more people to passionately and boldly speak my word."[14] Ouch! I didn't see that one coming. I didn't like that response, either, because it cut to the core of how we respond to the gift of life that God has given each of us and the adventure He has called us on during our life here on earth. Besides, if I were challenged to look at what it meant to lay down my life for Him and if I were going to take being a Christian seriously and start living the life I was called to live then I couldn't argue. Well, I could try.

There's a similar story in the Bible about someone who heard God call him to do something that made no sense whatsoever. Jonah ignored God's call to go to Nineveh and, as a result, found himself in several difficult positions, one of which was in the belly of a fish. Since I didn't want to spend time in the belly of a fish, I got really honest before God—as

---

[13] Isaiah 55:3 "Come to me with your ears wide open. Listen, for the life of your soul is at stake. I am ready to make an everlasting covenant with you." (NLT).

[14] Matthew 9:37–38 "He said to his disciples, "The harvest is great, but the workers are few. So pray to the Lord who is in charge of the harvest; ask him to send more workers into his fields." (NLT).

if you can hide anything from Him, anyway—and I admitted that I was not the academic kind and if He wanted me to go to school then I would try it on a "look see" basis. But He would have to write the exams and make sure that I passed and as long as I passed my courses then I would know that He did in fact want me to continue in school. Needless to say, on that particular day some of the scales fell from my eyes, and, so, following the direction of a friend of mine who said, "you'll never know if you don't at least try it," I stepped into the unknown, yet again.

I had not been given a permission slip to leave the room on Straight Street yet and as time went on God showed me warning signs that the partnership we had structured for the golf course was not God-ordained. Prior to structuring this partnership, I had never brought it before God for blessing and direction. In fairness, given where I was at in my own spiritual journey, I was not wise enough to bring it before God, but I now know that God's direction and guidance is foundational for everything I do.[15] I realized that if I stayed in the partnership it was headed for trouble and with that realization a large blanket of discouragement swept over me.[16] I talked with Deb about getting out of the golf course partnership and the whole concept about whether or not God wanted us in it at all. This level of communication was new for me and it brought a brand new dynamic in our own faith journey because this was an opportunity for us to really

---

[15] James 1:5 "If any of you lacks wisdom, he should ask God, who gives generously to all without finding fault, and it will be given to him." (NIV).

[16] Psalm 69:32 "Let all who seek God's help be encouraged." (NLT).

seek guidance together through prayer, God's word and the counsel from other brothers and sisters in Christ. So, while we're pushing in on this front, the comments from others about my going into ministry continued, adding a whole other dimension to our relationship. It was a big enough leap to even consider selling the dream, but going into the ministry as well?

Simply put, Deb hadn't signed up to marry a pastor. She did sign up to marry an entrepreneur, and this period was one of great adjustment for both of us. I take my hat off to her as she's not only a wonderful partner, but she has journeyed this road with me and there have been times when it has not been easy for her, either. Deb and I began to plan how we would go about selling our half of the corporation back to our partners and the potential of me going to school part-time to explore a Master of Divinity. This initial step was very painful. It turned our whole world upside down and brought me to my knees on many occasions. I had no sense of bearing and no past experience to draw upon. It turned Deb's world upside down, as well. We had many tears, words, and prayers as we tried to uncover what God was doing in our lives. Our whole world was changing around us and I felt like every time we got a sense of where things were going we were blindsided by another component of the call that we had not considered. I had many scales on my eyes.

We were being rewired and upgraded and it was hard. We sought the council of other people in the faith and we were very thankful for all of their support and prayers which covered us during this time of transition. But make no mistake about it, it's always harder for the person(s) who's entering the room on Straight Street than it is for those watching from the sidelines. The tendency in situations like this is to let one's mind worry about all the different implications and the endless list of things that could go wrong, and before you know it you're looking at a mountain of concerns, uncertainties, and worries with no solutions to any of them, and your focus is not on God's promise that He will look after you.[17] The tendency is to feel fear and total discouragement as you enter the room on Straight Street. Saul did. I did and you will.

It's always going to be easier to go your own way instead of entering the room with God and exploring what He has in mind for you. If you're going to try to the best of your abilities to live the life that God calls you to then you need to know that you'll be called to this room many times. My journey here is far from over, but if there is one key learning for me it's this—don't look at the many different obstacles, worries, excuses or reasons as to why you shouldn't go into the room. Rather ask yourself to look at the first item God used to get your attention with for the meeting on the Road to Damascus and that's usually where God wants to start His work in you. Ask Him to take away the distractions, to open your spiritual eyes and ears and to reveal the area in your life that He wants to rewire. Deal with what He reveals, first, one thing at a time and you'll find that a lot of the other

---

[17] Deuteronomy 31:8 "Do not be afraid or discouraged, for the LORD will personally go ahead of you. He will be with you; he will neither fail you nor abandon you." (NLT).

smaller ancillary worries will go away as you work on the one thing.

Jesus said the very same thing to Martha when he interrupted her and her sister Mary's daily life with a surprise visit. Martha gets totally freaked out about all the things that need to be done and the proper order in which to do them. She looks at all the obstacles and things that aren't being done properly. Martha's in the kitchen preparing everything according to the protocol of the day, while Mary has abandoned the confines of protocol and has decided to sit at the feet of Jesus, learning and soaking in every word. Martha finally flips out and demands that Jesus right the wrong here and tell her sister to get up and start helping with the to-do list. Can you feel the tension? Ever been there? We all have, but Jesus' words are key, here. He tells Martha that she mustn't be worried about the many things, but be solely focused on the one thing that He wanted to share with her as it can never be taken away.[18] The same is true for us in these moments. Focus on the one thing that God wants to share with you and let Him write it on your heart, forever.

This pattern has worked for me and continues to be an effective way of starting the upgrade process. I mentioned earlier that staying in the room on Straight Street involves

---

[18] Luke 10:38–42 "As they continued their travel, Jesus entered a village. A woman by the name of Martha welcomed him and made him feel quite at home. She had a sister, Mary, who sat before the Master, hanging on every word he said. But Martha was pulled away by all she had to do in the kitchen. Later, she stepped in, interrupting them. "Master, don't you care that my sister has abandoned the kitchen to me? Tell her to lend me a hand." The Master said, "Martha, dear Martha, you're fussing far too much and getting yourself worked up over nothing. One thing only is essential, and Mary has chosen it— it's the main course, and won't be taken from her." *The Message.*

pain, and for me the complete sacrifice and letting go of the dream was the most painful decision I'd ever had to make. I had to be vulnerable, humble, and trusting in His way, all the while letting Him work within me. God used this moment to begin a new thing in me and Deb, and it started with me giving up the worldly and focusing on the heavenly.[19] My internal rewiring at this stage centered on me giving up all of the benefits I associated with owning a golf course (prestige, power, money, control of my life) and surrendering them to God. It's hard to let go and completely trust when holding on makes us feel safe and secure.

I left my first visit to the room on Straight Street with the decision that we would step away from the golf course and I would explore going back to school on a part-time basis. Our attitude was in the event that if school didn't work out then at least the courses that I had taken would hopefully make me biblically smarter. Going back to school was never even on my radar, neither was it the pattern of the day, but Jesus decided to interrupt our daily routine because that's the way He works.

The call of Jesus starts with a small gentle whisper and gradually grows until such time as He steps into our daily routine of our comfort and interrupts us with such powerful force that it brings us to our knees. Nothing else matters when Jesus interrupts our lives. He does so to challenge our priorities, to turn our world upside down, to get our attention

---

[19] 1 Peter 2:11 "Friends, this world is not your home, so don't make yourselves cozy in it. Don't indulge your ego at the expense of your soul. Live an exemplary life among the natives so that your actions will refute their prejudices. Then they'll be won over to God's side and be there to join in the celebration when he arrives." *The Message.*

and to have us focus completely and entirely on His invitation to us. Oftentimes, the method in which the invitation of the call is delivered rattles our routines, but it gives us meaning in life, and just like Abraham who responded to the invitation and "followed the call of God without knowing where he was going. The people of Israel crossed a trackless desert following a pillar of cloud by day and a pillar of fire by night. In both cases, their sense of direction and meaning came solely from God's call, not from their foresight, their wisdom, or their ability to read their circumstances. They were on their way to a land of promise. They did not always know the way God was leading them, but they always knew why they trusted God: His word was the promise and his call was the way."[20] It's a custom-made invitation to a whole new world and a calling that He has chosen for each of us. No invitation is identical to another. There's a custom invitation made just for you and for me and its design is one that we would have never picked out for ourselves. It's specially created and very unique, just like you and me. The invitation reads:

To:	Insert your name here.
What is it:	Get together to discover your chosen destiny.
When is it:	Right here ... Right Now.
Where is it:	Starts in a room on Straight Street.
How do you get there:	Take my son's hand and trust me ...

---

[20] Os Guinness, *The Call—Finding and Fulfilling the Central Purpose of Your Life,* (Nashville, TN: Word Publishing, 1998), 178.

	I'll show you the way.
Why:	I chose to create you and I've
	called you to great things.
From:	Your Heavenly Father
Please R.S.V.P. by:	A.S.A.P.

Everyone responds differently to the invitation, usually in one of four categories. The first response is comprised of those who hear the call of Jesus and completely reject the invitation. Sadly, they choose a life totally separate and apart from any relationship with Him. These people are lonely, bitter, and contentiously unhappy.

I was getting some blood work done one day when a husband and wife walked into the waiting room. It was obvious that he was seriously ill and in a great deal of pain. It didn't take long to observe that he was very unhappy and afraid. He knew that he was staring death in the face. Every request or instruction for him to do something from the staff at the clinic was met with great anger and repetition of my Lord and Savior's name in vain. Clearly he did not have a relationship with Jesus Christ and maybe at this point in his life he was blaming God for the way things had turned out. His poor wife bore the brunt of his verbal attacks and it was obvious by the look in her eyes that she was really scared. So was he. Her husband's time on this earth was fast coming to an end and neither of them knew what lay ahead.

I'm convinced that the Bible is a historical account of God's pursuit of a relationship with each of us. It's unending, but there are those whom He has created and invited to join with Him in the greatest adventure, yet they have decided to decline the invitation and push God away. As time goes on, their pride blocks them from admitting that they've heard the call and they know that they've made a mistake by not accepting the invitation. Their disobedience to God's way has created a greater separation between them and God, and this separation has led to a hardheartedness that creates a wall of concrete around their soul and isolates them until they stare death in the face. By the time they hear death knocking at their door they feel it's too late to get it right with God, so they lash out at life out of great panic and fear that they have nowhere to turn for help because they've blocked out God's call for many years. They become too scared to reach out to Jesus at that point. They haven't even responded to the invitation with an R.S.V.P. That must break God's heart.

If this is your situation and you're reading this book and seeing yourself described here, please know that it's not too late to accept the invitation. God loves you and He's calling you to take the hand of His son, Jesus, and know that you're forgiven for ignoring Him all of these years. But don't wait any longer to accept the greatest invitation of all. Do it now.[21]

The second group are those who respond to the initial invitation to turn their lives over to Jesus Christ, but when they're called to go to the room on Straight Street, via the road to Damascus, they slowly shuffle their feet along that road going through the motions, filled with hesitation, very reluctant to fully embrace the room on Straight Street or any

---

[21] Romans 10:9 "That if you confess with your mouth, "Jesus is Lord," and believe in your heart that God raised him from the dead, you will be saved." (NIV)

teachings that Jesus has in store for them. They shuffle with small little steps, pretending, posing, saying all the right things, but never discovering anything new let alone putting their wholehearted trust in Jesus and the healing work He wants to do within them. Inch by boring inch, step by boring step, and with each repeated step a small part of them dies, refusing to acknowledge that "the only thing worse than dying is living a boring life."[22] They'll stay on the Road to Damascus never getting to the room on Straight Street, never discovering the real call on their life and never experiencing what it's like to walk with God.

The third group follows Jesus down the Road to Damascus and enters the room on Straight Street, but the initial pain experienced in this room keeps them frozen in fear and so they never leave the room. They never wait on God to bring the Ananias of their life into the room. The pain is so strong that they never really open their hearts to let God or others reach them so they never see what God has waiting for them: the discovery of their healing or comprehension of how much He thinks of them and loves them. They hold on to the pain and it builds up scales of resentment until eventually they just give up, feeling that if it can't be done their way, then this is as good as it gets. By staying in the room, they never see things with a new perspective and they never experience the full healing power of God.[23] They'll let God put in a new operating system, but they'll never learn how to fully use it. They'll either revert back to the old

---

[22] Marc Driscoll, *The Radical Reformation,* (Grand Rapids, MI: Zondervan, 2004), 14.

[23] See Acts 9:1–19

operating system, but stay in the room, never entrusting God with their heart as the pains and viruses of the past maintain their hold. They never experience freedom or healing.

Finally, the fourth group enters the room on Straight Street waiting for their Ananias to find them, waiting in the presence of God, learning and waiting on their Lord to teach them and rewire them to take action. As is always the case with God, He never forgets them and spends a great amount of time with them in that single room. Then, when God decides that they're ready, He sends an Ananias to be the catalyst for healing and the scales to fall off of their eyes and heart. They see things anew, they see things differently, and they can't wait to tell others about what Jesus did in their lives and what He can do for them.

As a result of their new perspective they know that Jesus will meet them again and will direct them back to the room on Straight Street where they'll enter the room with trepidation and excitement. Trepidation because they know that God has called them back here to work through some obstacles that are holding them back from experiencing the real adventure and love He has for them. They'll feel excitement, as well, because they know that God will fine tune their perspective and bring them back out of the room to participate in and discover His Kingdom here on earth to an even greater degree. The more times they trust God and let Him work in them, the greater the blessings.

You may be asking yourself, what does all of this have to do with God's call on my life and the answer is, everything! God calls us to the room on Straight Street so that His mission for our lives, the one that He has created for us in this life, is unleashed and becomes part of His kingdom here on Earth.[24] It's a powerful invitation that not everyone, even some Christians, respond to. It means that you will enter the room on Straight Street even if you don't know what's next or what it should look like or what the rules are. There will be critics, obstacles, temptations, and you'll feel like a vulnerable sitting duck with a huge target on your back. Entering that room for the first time will be the hardest thing you'll ever have to do. But if you're going to fully engage in the life that God has in store for you then you need the room on Straight Street.[25] It will change forever your understanding of who you are and who God is calling you to be. He's calling you to join Him on a journey of discovery. A journey that will wind in and out of the mountains and valleys of our lives. It won't be easy, but we must respond to the call if we are to reach God's destination for us and the story He's waiting and wanting to write for our lives. He's calling ... are you listening?

---

[24] Ephesians 2:10 "For we are God's workmanship, created in Christ Jesus to do good works, which God prepared in advance for us to do." (NIV).

[25] Warren *The Purpose Driven Life,* 42.

Chapter 7

A NEW AND IMPROVED WAY OF THINKING

"God will use circumstances to train you, but be ready to go in new directions as God leads you. Do not resist a change in direction." Sunday Andelaja

"And no one puts new wine into old wineskins. For the wine would burst the wineskins, and the wine and the skins would both be lost. New wine calls for new wineskins." Mark 2:22 NLT

Recently, our computer started acting up enough that I decided to invest in getting it properly fixed. When I got home I turned it on and it seemed to be good. I mean, there were no sparks or smoke coming out of the back of it and the window on my screen looked relatively familiar. Then out of nowhere pops a message stating that the computer no longer had anti-virus protection and was exposed to the big bad world of the Internet. After a short while, the anti-virus was reinstalled and I rebooted the machine with the assurance that I was protected from anyone intent on harming my computer. Once the anti-virus software was installed another message from my computer prompted me to do a deep system scan of all the files on the computer hard drive. It also recommended that I defrag my system.

For those of you who aren't computer literate, defragging is not a rude gesture. It's simply the computer's way of going through the files in the memory and reorganizing them so that the computer can run more efficiently. We're supposed to do it on a regular basis, but most of us don't take the time. These steps are very necessary and, for the most part, don't take a lot of time to complete, but by doing them the computer operates more efficiently.

The same is true with the time we spend in the room on Straight Street. God uses these moments to not only do a deep system scan of our lives and reveal anything that is a barrier in our relationship with Him (that's sin), but also to enhance our perspective and way of seeing things to be more closely aligned to His way, the way He wants us to see things (reordering how we store our internal files) in a heavenly perspective. This is where God rewires, redefines, and reawakens within us a new way of thinking, being, and doing. This is where He does a new thing, if—and it's a big IF—we're prepared to invest our time in the room with Him.

Part of my own deep system scan and defrag continued as I checked out the possibility of taking seminary courses on a part-time basis, as part of my plan to explore the whole concept of whether or not God was in fact calling me in this direction. Little did I know that God was going to reconfigure and reorganize my operating system in this process. He was going to expose me to a new way of thinking and as I walked through the doorway of the seminary to begin my very first day at school, I unknowingly re-entered the room on Straight Street. Had my upgrade/scan/defrag taken longer than I thought? Or, had I never left the room at all?

This period of time spent in school felt like an extended detention and was without a doubt one of the hardest things I had ever experienced up until then. I remember walking through the doors and feeling completely alone, out of my element, and acutely aware and afraid that my previous lack of scholastic desire and aptitude would soon be exposed. I was drenched in the perspiration of anxiety over the reality that in short order I would be annihilated in the ring of academic competition prevalent in any institution. I felt extremely vulnerable and ill-prepared. It's not that I didn't work on my scholastic portfolio the first time I went to University. No. I did work hard—well, sometimes, particularly on non-scholastic competitions. It didn't take long for me to figure out that the level of competition in a master's level was much higher. I felt like an elementary school kid being invited to try out for a high school team. I had no idea what the rules were and no previous experience to draw upon.

If I ran into a situation that I hadn't experienced before in the business world, I could rely on my street smarts and other past experiences to get me through. I knew what the rules of business were: to win, to beat everyone else, and to get the most toys. Those rules don't set you up very well in seminary. I had no idea what the written/unwritten rules were of either the church or the academic institution. I was completely blind and had no way of getting my bearings in this environment. The only person I could rely on while in the classroom was Jesus Christ and I began to really listen for his promptings and direction.

You may be saying to yourself, "Come on, it couldn't have been that bad on your first day at school. How unprepared were you?" I was so unprepared that I forgot to bring a Bible with me. Who forgets to bring a Bible with them on their first day of seminary? I realized it just minutes before my first class was to start and so I followed a string of arrows pointing to the library. I arrived at the library, trying my very best to pant as quietly as I could so as to not disturb anyone, and scanned the room for the librarian. She was sitting behind the "Information Desk."

I wandered over and, trying my best to breathe as quietly as I could, asked her how to go about taking out a book. She looked at me with a funny grin and pointed to the well-worn printed sheet of library rules taped to the top of her desk, implying that I should have already read these. Since I hadn't, I quickly scanned the rule sheet knowing that I didn't have the time to read, memorize, and begin living out these rules since my class was due to start any minute. With every ounce of guts I could find, I asked if she had a map that showed the different library sections. She said there were no maps like that and scolded me by saying that I should use one of the computers and follow the screens and promptings. Once I'd found the book I was looking for, I was to write down the code number and go into the room in the back of the library and find the book. By her tone I could tell she was wondering to herself what type of loser they let into the school this time. That didn't stop me, however, from continuing to pursue my goal of getting a Bible. It had now become a competition between me and the librarian.

Undeterred, I furrowed my eyebrows to look really determined and sure of what I was after and using my most intimidating scholastic "sure of what I want" voice I quietly asked her about the possibility that if knowing the title of the book would it make it easier and quicker to find its location within the library. Once again, she gave me that funny grin, but it was a little more painful this time, like she was trying to pass a kidney stone or something. She furrowed her eyebrows even more than I did and politely said that she could help me and show me how to follow the rules for finding a book. I offered a very enthusiastic and appreciative "that would be wonderful" to which she promptly walked over to the nearest computer. I don't know what it is about people who work in libraries, but they can sure move fast or perhaps she really did have a kidney stone.

Anyway, we got to the computer and she asks me for the title of the book that I want and I muffle under my breath that I was looking for a Bible.

"A what?" she replied, obviously ignoring standard library etiquette. Her facial reaction really did make me think that she was in fact starting to pass two kidney stones. After a quick pause, and realizing that everyone in the library had now heard her and was looking in our direction, her eyes wandered the room as if I was pulling her leg or looking for a hidden camera like she was on a television show. Then she looked at me and said, "Are you serious?" Talk about making a powerful first impression. She asked me what translation of Bible I needed.

"It doesn't really matter, but ... the right one would probably be good," I said.

"Follow me," she said then she was off like a baseball player trying to steal home plate at the bottom of the ninth and she represented the game winning run. It was all I could do to keep up with her. She handed me a Bible, told me to sign the card to take the Bible out. After doing so I smiled at her and thanked her so much for her help. But, I had one more question.

"Yes," she painfully replied, passing her third kidney stone.

"Where's the nearest exit out of here?"

She raised her hand with such authority I was expecting the walls to part, and left no doubt as to where the exit was. Realizing that class had now started and my time in the library had definitely run out, I grabbed the Bible from her as if it were a football and made like a running back trying to force his way through a quickly closing gap on a fourth and goal attempt, and literally ran out the exit to my classroom.

What a way to start seminary. I was smack dab in the middle of the room on Straight Street and I had no idea as to the layout of the room, how to get around the room or what type of obstacles awaited me while I spent time in the room. I was a fish out of water. That happens with our time in the room. We're made to fully rely on God so that He can teach us new perspectives in moments like these.[1]

---

[1]   Psalm 33:18 "But the Lord watches over those who fear him, those who rely on his unfailing love." (NLT)

God's defragging process not only gives us new perspectives, but requires a lot of reworking within. It's the rewiring of our internal processing unit. Everything we have come to understand as solid building blocks for our lives, the foundations upon which we plant our feet shift. God broadens the scope of our vision and calls us to be open to considering other elements that we might not necessarily have thought of before. It's not meant to be superficial or shallow, but rather transformational for us so that we walk away from the experience not only changed but also affirmed with His direction for our lives. God begins to condition us spiritually so that we learn to rely more on His promptings, hear His voice and participate in His Kingdom here on Earth instead of what man says we should do. So, when God defrags our being, He gets rid of earthly attachments and idols. He begins the process of cleaning house inside each of us all the while running a deep system scan of any man-made viruses that might have attached themselves to us. He puts new wine into new wine skins. He starts—just like He did with Saul—by stripping away our ego. That's the part of us that has a tendency to Edge God Out (EGO) of our lives.

If we never let God do a deep system scan of our lives, we will never get a chance to fully realize the God-given capacity and life that he has planned for us. Many people when they become Christians just let God do a preliminary scan of their lives and leave it at that. That was me. I knew that I had received forgiveness and believed that Jesus died for my sins, and once I had accepted him as my Lord and Savior there wasn't anything else I needed to do. Many people call themselves Christians and are stalled at that stage in their spiritual journey. As long as God doesn't go really deep into the past and reveal things long-buried in the dark recesses of our memory, as long as He doesn't ask them to deal with all of that pain, then things will be fine. It's easier to just let God stay on the surface, but the reality is that He already knows what we've done in the past, every last thing, and He already knows the viruses that we've let into our lives. He just wants to see if we'll trust Him enough to have Him reveal all of our past and to surrender it to His healing touch. The real question asked of us during our time in the room on Straight Street is whether or not we'll let God do a deep system scan and really heal us of our past.

Letting God do the work He wants to do in us means that we won't get any critical error screens. You know, the window that pops up and announces that the upgrade was unsuccessful due to a critical error and then lists string of code that makes no sense as to where or what went wrong. When that happens we freeze with fear then respond by pushing the cancel button just to end the upgrade process, and return our computer to the state is was in before the attempted upgrade. It's the same with our lives and it's human nature to avoid having to deal with such issues. We love to deal in generalities where we can just stay on the surface where it's safer and easier. Revealing the issues around our hearts would open up too much pain and we would lose control of the outcome so, when God calls us to the room to draw us closer to Him, strengthen our relationship with Him and to upgrade our lives, we create a wall that stops the defrag and deep system scan of our lives. Pride and fear hold us back from letting God reveal the big issues/items that we need to work on to broaden our perspective, upgrade our systems, and free us from the sin that's preventing us from operating at the capacity that God created for us and has called us to experience. It is during these moments in the room on Straight Street that God prompts us to let Him complete a deep scan of our lives and reveal the areas that we need to let go of and work on, and to reorganize our priorities.

The process of a deep system scan and defrag has different levels of pain associated with it. To be free from pain we must embrace those moments of revelation so God can start the healing process. If we're not aware of the specifics and why they're rooted in the pain we won't be able hand them over to Him.

I'm reminded of the day my wife decided that we were going to paint the living room.

"Honey, do you think that today is the day we should paint the living room?"

I quickly scanned my mind for the deep and profound theological answer, "Yes, dear."

As we completed the to-do list of things we needed to successfully redo our living room, we followed our normal routine, which included putting our dog in her crate before we left the house. When we returned, we set the painting materials on the floor then I went into our room to change into painting clothes. Moments later, the quiet stillness of the morning was broken with the sound of a dog howling and my wife screaming my name.

In her excitement at having us home, our dog had stepped on a loose wire in her crate, which we hadn't noticed. Every time the dog tried to pull her paw away from the wire it became further embedded in her paw which would add to the decibel level of her howl. To free her, we had to push the wire further into her paw so that we could bend the wire in such a way that it would allow us to release her. I grabbed hold of her paw to minimize the pain, but additional pain was required to free her. If someone had come into the room during this escapade without knowing anything about what had led up to this event, they would have viewed it as me hurting the dog, when in fact we were actually freeing her from the pain that was holding her captive. The same is true in our own lives when God does a deep system scan and reveals areas in our lives that we need to bring to Him. It's not God's nature to want to hurt us, but it is in His nature to free us from sin in our lives so that we can live a life of freedom in His presence.[2]

These types of experiences lead us to new perspectives, new territories and a new way of thinking, and they take us out of our comfort zone. The four years I spent in seminary— it seemed like forty—were incredibly challenging for me and my family. The total encompassing grace of God, support of family, friends and a church community made the experience manageable, and God used this time to do a deep system scan and a complete defrag of my life and paradigm. With each challenge and obstacle I overcame, more scales on my eyes fell away. With every new friendship made and new

---

[2] Jeremiah 30:17 "'I will restore you to health and heal your wounds,'" declares the LORD." (NIV).

experience encountered (positive or negative), a few more scales would fall from my eyes. With the letting go of our portion of the golf course and the breaking of my reliance on money, a few more scales fell from my eyes. Some of these experiences were incredibly painful and others were joyful surprises, but with each one, God removed more scales from my eyes just like the patient who has had eye surgery and waits with great anticipation for the surgeon to eventually remove the bandages around their eyes so that they can see. As the bandages come off, there's that period of white fuzzy haze as their eyes adjust to the new light. That's the outcome of time spent in the room on Straight Street and I was fully and completely relying on God's victorious right hand to guide me through until all the scales had fallen off my eyes.[3]

God always follows through for those who step out to answer His call to spend time in the room. In the last chapter I spoke about my request that if God were calling me to go to seminary then I needed Him to walk ahead of me while at school and take care of my marks. During my first semester about a month before my New Testament exam, the professor announced that at the end of class she would have available nine sample essay questions to help us prepare for the upcoming exam. She told us that the exam would have only two essay questions on it and they would come from these nine sample questions. She then advised us that to prepare for the exam

---

[3]   Isaiah 41:10 "Don't be afraid, for I am with you. Don't be discouraged, for I am your God. I will strengthen you and help you. I will hold you up with my victorious right hand." (NLT).

we should do at minimum five of these questions, but to be safe we should really do seven. However, in the event that anyone was so inclined, and for the challenge of it, we could do all nine to cover all the bases. She then suggested that our studying efforts would be more effective if we formed study groups where we allocated one question to each of the group's participants and then share our answers with the rest of the group. It would minimize the work required and would make people feel like they're part of a team/community.

I started to map out in my mind how I could go about getting into one of the study groups. I never got the opportunity to explore this concept further as the next time our class met everyone had already formed their study groups and assigned questions. I realized very quickly that I was going to be preparing for this exam all alone. I knew I would need help. I quickly reminded God that He was to take care of the marks for me and I asked Him to lead me in my preparation for the exam. After a period of quiet reflection on all the questions offered for the exam I felt guided towards two particular questions out of the nine and so, because of time restrictions—I was still running my consulting business—I only prepared for two questions.

The day of the exam arrived and I was nervous, edgy, and just wanting the whole painful thing to be done. As I entered the examination room some of the academic keeners had already staked their turf near the front of the classroom and were talking with the professor about how many questions they answered in preparation for the exam. Most of them had done all nine. Go figure! But as the professor went around the room asking each person how many questions they'd done in preparation she finally got to me. I couldn't lie and so when she asked me I merely responded that I'm a bit of a risk taker and I only did two. Well you should have seen the look on her face (and the look on the other students' faces). A huge silence fell over the entire room. I quickly looked at my watch and added that since we still had ten minutes before the exam started I thought it would be a great time to go to the chapel and pray. So I excused myself and left the room. Boy, did I pray. I told God that I needed the questions I had studied to be on the exam.[4] And I trusted that God was going to deliver. I returned to the room in time to receive the exam. I knew that the professor was looking for my facial reaction when I opened the exam. As I looked at the questions, low and behold the two I studied for were on the exam. I wanted to jump up on the desk and yell, "Yes!!" God is so good.

I had successfully passed my first academic test in seminary. The sad truth of the matter is that it didn't take long for me to lose focus on what had just happened here. As much as I was very thankful that God had answered my prayer pertaining to passing the exam, my own human nature started to reveal its prideful side when one day while walking to class I was talking to a spiritual mentor of mine and I started to boast about all the sacrifices I was making to verify God's potential call here to seminary. The voice on the other end of the phone brought me back down to reality.

"Norman, God doesn't want your sacrifices. He wants

---

[4]   Luke 11:10 "Don't bargain with God. Be direct. Ask for what you need." *The Message.*

more than that."

This got my attention real quick and it felt like God was stepping into my life and slapping me upside the head with a holy jolt, another wake up call and reality check. Surely God would be impressed with everything I and my family had given up and sacrificed to get to this point. My mentor told me that sacrificing was a good start, but we'd never be in a position to equal or match the greatest sacrifice of all time—that being what Jesus did on the cross for us. He sacrificed His life so we could have a relationship with the heavenly Father.[5] The voice on the other end of the phone drilled down a little bit further.

"You'll never impress God with all that you've sacrificed for Him because this journey calls us to actually go past keeping score of what you've sacrificed and step into learning how to live a life of obedience." Perhaps that was the first major learning of my time in the room on Straight Street. Some of the scales over my eyes were rooted in my ledger of sacrifice by keeping score of everything I had given up to answer His call. I had been stuck in a sacrificial mode wanting to impress others, including God, with all that I and my family had sacrificed.

Looking back at the computer analogy, whenever my computer finishes a deep system scan it always prompts me with issues that it found during the scan that need to be dealt with. It also provides me with the prompting to deal with them

---

[5]   John 3:16–17 "For God loved the world so much that he gave his one and only Son, so that everyone who believes in him will not perish but have eternal life. God sent his Son into the world not to judge the world, but to save the world through him." (NLT).

now or not. Accept or decline. Yes or no. The same is true in our relationship with God and the time we spend with Him in the room on Straight Street. He will find things in our lives that need to be addressed and we will always be asked if we want to deal with them or not. Accept or decline. Yes or no.

I knew that if I was to grow in my relationship with God, and others, I was being called to deal with and get rid of this file called "ledger of sacrifice." My perspective had changed and reorganization of my internal files was needed. New wine was being poured into a new wineskin for my life. My perspective had broadened and God had used the first part of seminary to show me that I could stay in this mode and join many others and remain stuck here, never learning or advancing in their spiritual journey or, I could learn from it by attempting to draw closer to God to see what He was trying to do in me. It was the beginning of no longer looking at what I had incurred, given up or relinquished, and the start of my refocusing on what God wanted me to learn, experience and grow.

Is God prompting you of issues in your life that need to be addressed? Perhaps you've been keeping some sort of ledger with God and He now wants to clean the slate and balance the account. If that's the case I urge you to go with it and find out what He's trying to teach you. Learn from it, grow with it and in the words of Jesus learn what you can expect from yourself. "Anyone who intends to come with me has to let me lead. You're not in the driver's seat—I am. Don't run from suffering; embrace it. Follow me and I'll show you how. Self-help is no help at all. Self-sacrifice is the way, my way, to finding yourself, your true self. What good would it do to get everything you want and lose you, the real you?"[6]

---
[6] Luke 9:23 *The Message*

Chapter 8

TRUST TRUMPS JUST

The story is told of a mother who is busy in the kitchen preparing a festive family meal and she invites her daughter to learn how to cook the ham just the way her grandma taught her.

"I think you're old enough to learn this secret recipe," says the mother.

The daughter responds with an enthusiastic, "yes," and

wraps herself up with one of her mom's aprons. She pulls up a nearby stool to the island counter where her mother is preparing all of the other elements for the meal. With great anticipation she climbs each step of the stool and puts her little hand on the guiding arm of her mom all the while looking with great awe at what lay before her. What little child doesn't love to play with cooking stuff? The mother looks at the child with a big smile and tells her that many years ago her mom invited her to help prepare the festive meal when she was the very age she is. The mom further prefaces the wisdom she is about to pass on by saying that the daughter should never deviate from the traditional cooking instructions and should pay attention to what she was about to see so she could pass the recipe on when she grew up.

With eyes the size of giant gumballs, the daughter looks at her mom and nods. "I will, I will for sure, Mom." And so the mother imparts a family secret which is now passed from one generation to the other, embedded in the memory of that little child.

"First, you cut the ham in half," the mother begins, then outlines each specific spice and all of the subsequent cooking instructions. The meal is a success and the mom and dad both compliment their daughter on her new-found cooking abilities.

Years go by and the little girl grows up, gets married and is blessed with a daughter of her own. Not forgetting that special moment with her mom, the time comes when she invites her daughter to help her prepare the festive family meal and to learn great-grandma's recipe for cooking the ham. As her little girl crawls up the stool beside the counter, holding onto her mom's arm she looks with great anticipation at everything before her. All the while the mother is looking at her daughter and remembering exactly how she felt that day when her mom passed on the family tradition.

"First, you cut the ham in half," she said, then outlines each specific spices and all of the subsequent cooking instructions.

The little girl quickly interrupts her mom. "Mom, how come you cut the ham in half?"

The mother looks at the girl a little bewildered and says, "It's just the way we do it," and continues to explain the rest of the recipe.

The little girl interrupts, again. "But, Mom, it doesn't make any sense why you cut the ham in half."

The mom responds with a little more edge to her reply, "That's just the way we do it."

When the little girl asks a third time, the mother replies that she should ask her grandmother and great-grandmother that question when they joined them for dinner. That was good enough for the little girl and so she watched and learned the rest of the recipe in silence.

Later that night, the little girl's grandmother arrives and before the grandmother had even sat down the little girl asked, "Grandma, how come you cut the ham in half before you cook it?"

Looking a little perplexed the grandmother looked over to the girl's mother for an explanation.

The mother replied, "Today, I shared the family recipe for how to cook the family ham. And our little miss was wondering why we cut the ham in half before we cook it. I couldn't answer with anything that satisfied her so I told her to ask either you or great-grandmother when you arrived."

"Humph, I don't know why," the grandmother said. "All I know is that my mom passed the recipe on to me and you never deviate from the recipe. You never change things. You always cut the ham the exact same way and you cook the ham the exact same way. You always do it the same way. It's just part of our tradition." The grandmother and mom nodded, confirming each other's belief that their answer had satisfied the little girl's curiosity. It didn't satisfy the little girl at all and so they waited until great-grandmother arrived. The little girl asked her great-grandmother the same question.

By now the little girl's father had joined the group and wondered exactly how the entire mystery was going to unfold. There were three generations waiting with great anticipation at the great-grandmother's wisdom that was about to be shared.

The great-grandmother replied, "Well that's easy, it was the only way I could make the ham fit in the pan that I used to cook it." That answer made total sense to the little girl who then hugged her great-grandmother and went off to play. Mystery solved. Here were two generations that had never deviated from the recipe/plan because they assumed that it always had to be done that way and they themselves had remained stuck in the pattern of doing things a particular way.

The same can be said with how we do church, how we train/teach future church leaders in seminary, how we transition leadership within the church from one generation to another and how we live our daily lives. The same is true with how God calls us and our response to that call. We miss too many of His calls by being stuck in the pattern of "it's just the way we do it." The response that "God's always done it this particular way and He never does it differently" is not true nor is it biblical. Yet to this group it is very clear that if someone else is sensing God calling them to do something that has either never been done before or is done differently than before or in a manner completely contrary to how they believe God does things, well then they must be a troublemaker and for sure they must be wrong. People get stuck in this stage of their spiritual journey and they never leave it, they never grow outside the boundaries of "it's just the way we do it."

The phone conversation mentioned in the previous chapter was a major awakening for me as I realized that I was stuck in this spot using my "look what I've given up for you, God" response (keeping a ledger of sacrifice) rather than being fully open to what He was trying to teach me. But I also noticed that many people in the seminary and church were also stuck in this spot.

The religious elite of Jesus' day had the same disease and they too were stuck, never knowing the excitement of fully answering God's call on their lives. Throughout the book of Matthew,[1] Jesus shook the status quo of life. The only habit he maintained was taking quiet time to pray and listen for his heavenly Father's direction. Following Jesus was a new adventure that entailed healing people from the disease of

---

[1] Matthew 3:1–12, Matthew 9:14–17, 12:1–8,

"sacrificial stuckitis."[2] People suffering from this disease are exposed by their reliance on their head knowledge without engaging their heart's ownership and acting on what it really means to follow Jesus Christ. They say the right things, but never step out into the unknown. They "have the letter without the heartbeat. They can accurately repeat chapter or verse, but they have lost the breath of life behind the Scriptures."[3] Freeing ourselves from the symptom of "sacrificial stuckitis" means that we must stop patting ourselves on the back for all the things we've given up or sacrificed so we can call ourselves Christians and really make ourselves available to hearing God's voice and then obey His calling.[4] God is full of surprises and never steps into our lives the same way every time. This way, we don't get stuck in the pattern of predictability or the danger of thinking that we know exactly how God moves to get our attention.

When Seth Godin and his family arrived in France on a vacation, they were totally enchanted with the beautiful countryside and the cows that filled the pastures. "Within twenty minutes, we started ignoring the cows. The new cows were just like the old cows, and what was once amazing was now common. Worse than common. It was boring."[5] The only thing that could change their dullness was if someone had placed one purple cow amidst all of the other cows.

---

[2] Matthew 12:7 " ... I don't want your sacrifices ... " (NLT).

[3] John Bevere, *Under Cover — The Promise of Protection Under His Authority,* (Nashville, TN: Thomas Nelson, 2001), 39.

[4] 1 Samuel 3:10 "The Lord came and stood there, calling as at other times, "Samuel! Samuel!" Then Samuel said, "Speak for your servant is listening." (NASB)

[5] Seth Godin, *The Purple Cow,* (New York, NY: Penguin Group, 2003), 3.

That purple cow would have drawn their attention from the predictable and boring. Predictability blinds us and hinders our ability to see and hear God's call to get our attention. God speaks to us in ways that are unpredictable and requires us to be aware of the many different ways He may pursue us. The sad reality is that many of us miss what He's got in store because we're content to stay at the sacrificial and predictable level. We never move to the deeper level of living our lives by way of obedience.

God is not into the status quo, but rather He moves throughout the World touching lives in many different ways. If we stay blinded by and suffering from "sacrificial stuckitis" we'll miss out on the greater and more rewarding experiences that await our obedience to whatever God calls us to do. God does not want our sacrifices, but wants us to be obedient to His calling and grow deeper with Him.[6] When we sacrifice our self-perceived, over-inflated sense of strength, our need for control, approval, applause—you fill in the blank—and respond to His voice by letting God access our lives at a different level than before, we experience something brand new and our spiritual senses become more in tune to hearing His voice.

God is not a god of pattern or routine. Rather, He calls us to give up the perceived importance of our sacrifices, and step into a new dimension of obedience and thrive in holy submission that can only come from life-changing

---

[6] 1 Samuel 15:22 "Samuel replied, "What is more pleasing to the Lᴏʀᴅ: your burnt offerings and sacrifices or your obedience to his voice. Obedience is far better than sacrifice. Listening to him is much better than offering the fat of rams." (NLT).

participation with Him. It's not about you or me. It's about finding out what we're willing to let go of and let God do through us. What recipes/traditions/stories are we passing down to the next generation and are they the recipes that will inspire and motivate them to answer God's voice and change the World?

It is my sincere hope that my wife and I will have lived our lives in such a way that our children will be able to remember, and then share with their children, the different stories of our attempts to answer God's call. My years in seminary provided a vast inventory of stories that my family has participated in with me. The stories covered the gamut of emotions from funny to sad, exciting to extremely hurtful and this particular chapter was completed on the night of my graduation. This was one chapter that gave an example for my children to witness the effort it takes to respond to God's call.

For our family, it was the completion of a chapter in our lives and the beginning of the new one. For my wife and me, it was the shift into a deeper level of obedience in our relationship with Jesus Christ. I had learned so much about myself, people, the institution of the church, God and who He was calling me to be. This period was my own personal transition from sacrifice (look at everything I've given up for you Jesus) to obedience (Lord, you must be in this as you've never failed me. Even when people deliberately tried to do evil things to me, you, Lord, used it for good[7]). Every event that God invited me to participate in, whether

---

[7]   Genesis 50:20 " ... You planned evil against me but God used those same plans for my good" *The Message*.

it was enjoyable or not, was an opportunity to experience something brand new and to learn something about myself, others, and God.

These right here ... right now moments are new adventures that broaden our horizons as we learn whatever it is that He's trying to teach us, and rarely, if ever, are they done in a predictable way. If Jesus was not predictable in His ways and He, and the example set by the disciples, is the best example for being the church, then perhaps we should ask the question, why are so many churches and their leadership continuing to suffer from sacrificial stuckitis? Why are they so opposed to new ideas and doing new things when the very God we worship is all about creating brand new ways to experience Him? He calls us to not be embarrassed, or to hold back, but to think big,[8] so why do many churches do the opposite? Maybe it's time that we changed the pattern and freed ourselves from being stuck in the quagmire of sacrifice, and answer God's call to step into a whole new way of living ... obedience.

The Bible contains many examples where God has called, equipped, encouraged, and empowered people to step outside of their sacrificial stuckitis by inviting them to participate in events that defied all sensibilities. Those who answered the call could look back on the experience with great awe at how God had moved through them to do something amazing, and then retell the story to future generations. Below is a partial list of those stories where God called people to do something that made no sense:

---

[8]   Isaiah 54:1–6 *The Message*.

- God speaks to Moses through a burning bush and then advises him that He will lead the Israelites out of slavery (Exodus 3).
- God guides the Israelites by pillars of cloud and fire (Exodus 13).
- God uses a talking donkey to get Balaam's attention (Numbers 22).
- God uses dreams to speak to Joseph (Genesis 37).
- God sends angels to speak with Mary (Luke 1).
- God sends his son Jesus to come into the world and speak to us (Hebrews 1).
- Jesus calls out and tells Peter to walk on the water with him (Matthew 14).
- God calls Abraham to leave the land he was in (routine of comfort) and to go by faith into the unknown (Genesis 12).

None of these happenings or invitations by God made sense to the invited at the time. They were outside of the way things had always been done. That's God's way. He's full of surprises, and through all of those surprises, His plan is to heal us from sacrificial stuckitis and to invite us to the many opportunities of obedience.

God invites all of us to do things that make no sense, and if we really want to walk the walk we're called to, sooner or later, we have to step out and follow Him to get unstuck and grow deeper in our relationship with Him. Is God calling you to do something that makes no sense to get you unstuck from something in your life? If so, how are you going to answer?

Nate Saint was a missionary who, along with four

others, was killed by the Auca Indians in Ecuador when they attempted to establish a relationship with this remote tribe so they could share Jesus Christ with them. He said that his "life did not change until he came to grips with the idea that obedience is not a momentary option. It is a die-cast decision made beforehand."[9] Spending time in the room on Straight Street means that we will be given a choice as to whether we're going to answer God's call to grow in obedience or stay stuck in sacrifice.

Upon my graduation from the seminary, God invited me and my family to go to a deeper level of spiritual growth, one of obedience, and it took me a while to see that He was calling in a different direction than any of our own desires might have been.

This particular call started a year before graduation when I was invited to speak at Lakeshore St. Andrew's Presbyterian Church near Windsor, Ontario, which is located just across the river from Detroit, Michigan. It's a large, vibrant, and growing church that God has blessed throughout its history in the Windsor area. My first opportunity to speak there was a wonderful experience and they made me and my family feel incredibly welcome. The five-hour car ride home after that particular Sunday gave Deb and I plenty of time to talk about our visit. The conversation finished with Deb saying that it was a nice place to visit, but she "was never moving to Windsor."

With my final year of school and subsequent graduation

---

[9] Michael P. Green, *1500 Illustrations for Biblical Preaching,* (Grand Rapids, MI: Baker Books, 2000), 253.

successfully completed, the next question was, "What's next Lord?" At the time I didn't really feel a strong call towards church ministry, but in the event that God was calling me to do so, I knew that I didn't want to be the lead pastor, but rather the associate where I could watch and observe. There were a couple of local options that might work, and while I would publicly say that I was keeping my doors open to whatever God was leading, the reality was that I was open to being obedient as long as God kept us where we were currently living. Our family used this time to visit a vast number of churches in the area who were all doing different styles of ministry, and it was a great learning experience for me as I was able to see firsthand how I could use different elements from each one of the services and combine them to do something brand new. One option we considered was planting a church, and I began to look at a variety of different locations that could possibly work out. I kept putting out resumes into the corporate world, too, while keeping my eye on two particular local church options that I could see myself being called to. Our prayer was simply that God would open the door to where He wanted us to be and soundly close the doors to those options that He did not want us to walk through. A simple yet powerful prayer.

In short order, God very definitively closed the doors to the two local options. One of the churches was being called to risk the allocation of their resources to fund an additional service/new format and create a new evangelical worship style to reach the unreached in their community. The plan was to borrow the necessary funds from their substantial endowment fund, which had well over a million dollars in it, and eventually pay the funds back once the new format was viable and generating enough offerings. This concept caused a major split in the church and sadly they chose not to step out in faith and follow God's call to risk doing something brand new, and so the whole plan was kyboshed. It became very apparent that they loved their bricks, mortar, and organ more than they loved the unreached in their community, so God closed that door for me as a possible option. In regards to the other option, God opened our spiritual eyes and made it very clear that it was not where He wanted us to be. Unfortunately, it, too, had gone through some real heartache and had split, as well.

I had also started the necessary paperwork to establish a charitable ministry that would use worship events to unify the church body. It, too, became apparent that the timing for this was not right and so with an open hand I gave it back to God knowing that He might call me to do something like this in the future, but not at that moment. I looked at planting a new church by beginning a small home church. While this experience was great, God started to show both Deb and me that if we were to continue, and given the turmoil going on in the other two churches, it would cause further division within the body so we stopped it and really started to push in on hearing from God as to what and where He was calling us.

Meanwhile, Lakeshore St. Andrew's had gone through a leadership transition and had begun looking to fill the position of the Associate Pastor. They touched base with me on a regular basis to see how I was making out and to prompt me to consider putting my name in for this position. The first couple of times I discounted it and politely said "no, thank you," even though my past experience with the church said it was healthy and a good model. Ten months after graduation, there was still no job and not one single interview from the fifty-plus resumes I had sent out to companies in the corporate world. God was continuing to honor our prayer by speaking through open and closed doors ... and there was really only one door left open. One afternoon, God moved by way of further opening this door when Deb said she would follow wherever, and if Windsor was where God was calling us to go then we should check it out.

The next day we invited good friends of ours over to discuss the Windsor idea and they said we'd never know if we didn't explore it. Other advice, both from strong believers and those who were not, either said, "you're nuts" or "why not?" So, after some real quiet time with God, I had to know if this was the door He was holding open, and so I put my hat in the ring for the position in Windsor. Funny how things work, God's vision and path for us wasn't the way we initially expected it to be, but before we knew it we were selling our house, leaving the community that we had called home for so many years, and heading to a location and position that none of us ever expected. My wife now says in no uncertain terms that she is never moving to Hawaii!!!

In this whole period of transition for our family, God answered so many specific prayers that our stepping out in faith was a wonderful example to our kids and even though there were hard moments in the move, we were able to see

God prepare the path down to Windsor in such a way that none of us thought were possible, expected or foreseen.[10] Hindsight is always 20/20, and it is much easier to sit on the other side of transition and look back upon all of the events that affirm the decision to act in faith than to see the results at the time of stepping out. That's what faith is all about, stepping out and trusting in God without knowing the exact details of what awaits.

Our journey to Windsor started with looking for places to live and as we looked at all of the different areas to choose from, our kids asked that they not have to take anymore school buses. As we investigated further we found one area where we would be within walking distance of a brand new elementary and high school. That was a direct answer to prayer. Not only would our kids not have to take a school bus, but they wouldn't be the only "new kids." They would turn out to be fantastic schools and wonderful experiences for both our kids.

The school issue solved, we moved on to finding a house in the area. There were many choices to buy, but since our house back in Barrie had not sold, yet, we began to look at what was available in the area for rent. We were surprised that given the tough economic conditions there wasn't much available. But, trusting that God would show us His way for this obstacle, I called each private for-sale property asking them if they wanted to rent. The answers kept coming back, "No, we don't want to rent," but I was not going to quit and

---

[10] 1 Corinthians 2:9 "No eye has seen, No ear has heard, no mind has conceived what God has prepared for those who love him." (NIV).

eventually one owner put me in touch with another owner who he thought would be interested in renting.

When I first approached him, he said he didn't want to rent, but wanted to sell and he forwarded me a complete marketing brochure of the house, including many pictures, with the hopes that it would persuade me to buy instead of rent. It was a beautiful house (we called it the Pastor Palace) and when I showed Deb and the kids the pictures they were really excited that such a house was available. However, once they found out that he wasn't interested in renting their enthusiasm waned. We decided that we would pray every night for the owner to change his mind, and so we did. Every night we prayed that God would change his heart and let us rent the house. One evening our daughter finished the prayer with, "Lord, please let us rent Bill's house, please, Bill. Amen, Bill." From that point on we added, "Bill, Amen, Bill." Well, God honored that prayer and set us up in a great house to rent, then sold our house back home allowing us to build a new home in our new community where we could put roots down. (Bill wasn't his real name. We've just changed it to protect his current tenants from starting to pray for lower rent.)

One of my son's prayers was to make the school basketball team. His new school had a very strong athletic program and even though he's a very good basketball player, it was difficult cracking into an established group of players. God answered his prayer with not only making the team, but eventually making the starting five and then being chosen to represent his school in the all-city team. This was just one of the prayers that God answered for my son and a powerful witness for him to see firsthand how God takes care of those who step out in faith and obedience.

Deb got onto the supply list for teachers in the Windsor Essex school board. We didn't know at the time just how difficult that was, but God had rallied a few prayer partners together in that area and He answered that prayer. We found out later that a lot of people had been waiting years just to get on the supply list. Every morning Deb would wait for the phone to ring, take the job offered and go off to a new school. Every day felt like the first day of school for her, and while she was very appreciative of the job it was a challenging change for her since she was used to going to the same school with the same staff and knowing most of the kids. Eventually God answered another prayer by giving her a long-term occasional position where she would fill in for someone who was on maternity leave for a semester. This meant that she would be stationed in the same school and would get to know the staff and students. While the job transition in moving to Windsor was hard, the experience made her a better teacher and more aware of others who were going through the same challenges.

My daughter's prayers included making new friends very easily and fitting in at her new school. God answered that right away as she made many new friends and was selected to represent all of the schools within our county area in a leadership development camp put on by the Ontario Provincial Police. It was nice to see how God affirmed her leadership gifts in such a powerful and enjoyable way.

The community of Lakeshore St. Andrew's did a wonderful

job of welcoming us to the church and the greater community. I can't say enough about how they walked with us through all of the challenges of us moving down and then welcoming someone new to their church family. It didn't take long at all for me to feel like I fit in and I was blessed by the many opportunities that presented themselves to learn from so many talented and wise people. I was able to step right into a very healthy church model and learn so much, so quickly.

As we looked back on the way things unfolded, we realized we would never have written the script for the move to Lakeshore the way it turned out. We never anticipated the split that would happen in our church back home, and yet God's plan called us out of that area before any of that had happened and put us into a healthy place where we could worship and learn firsthand about a model of ministry that worked. Rob's basketball team back home had a brutal year and yet Rob's experience in Windsor was the exact opposite. Kristina was involved in power cheerleading before we moved and if we had stayed and she were to move to the next level she'd have had to learn how to tumble. When we moved to Windsor there was no cheerleading available in the area, but she was able to find a great gymnastics club where she learned how to tumble.

Just before we moved down to Windsor, I prayed that my van with over 150,000 miles on it would get us safely down the highway to Windsor. Well, it's been almost twenty-four months since making that prayer and as I sit and write about it, the van is parked in the garage with almost 210,000 miles on it and has survived several trips. God has answered that prayer and then some.

These are just some of the prayers that God answered. This move was a time of spiritual shifting and learning about the whole concept of obedience. We had never before in our lives stepped out to such a great degree, and this shifting from sacrificial stuckitis to taking advantage of the opportunity of obedience is hard, uncomfortable, and usually happens when we're right in the middle of doing the normal and comfortable routines of life.

Perhaps the biggest lesson in shifting from sacrifice to obedience was developing my aptitude for really trusting God. Jesus says in John 14:11, "Believe Me that I am in the Father and the Father in Me; or else believe Me for the sake of the [very] works themselves. [If you cannot trust Me, at least let these works that I do in My Father's name convince you]" (AMP). He tells us this so that we can be assured that the results we see when we step out in faith help develop and strengthen our ability to shift from sacrifice stuckitis to thriving in obedience. The Bible is full of those who stepped out. We don't read about those who were stuck in fear or sacrifice their whole lives never really taking advantage of the opportunity of obedience. We do, however, read about those who do step out of their comfort zone and obediently answer God's call to pursue him. Consider Peter and the gang of fishermen in Luke 5:1–11.

> [1-3]Once when he was standing on the shore of Lake Gennesaret, the crowd was pushing in on him to better hear the Word of God. He noticed two boats tied up. The fishermen had just left

them and were out scrubbing their nets. He climbed into the boat that was Simon's and asked him to put out a little from the shore. Sitting there, using the boat for a pulpit, he taught the crowd.

[4]When he finished teaching, he said to Simon, "Push out into deep water and let your nets out for a catch."

[5-7]Simon said, "Master, we've been fishing hard all night and haven't caught even a minnow. But if you say so, I'll let out the nets." It was no sooner said than done—a huge haul of fish, straining the nets past capacity. They waved to their partners in the other boat to come help them. They filled both boats, nearly swamping them with the catch.

[8-10]Simon Peter, when he saw it, fell to his knees before Jesus. "Master, leave. I'm a sinner and can't handle this holiness. Leave me to myself." When they pulled in that catch of fish, awe overwhelmed Simon and everyone with him. It was the same with James and John, Zebedee's sons, coworkers with Simon.

[10-11]Jesus said to Simon, "There is nothing to fear. From now on you'll be fishing for men and women." They pulled their boats up on the beach, left them, nets and all, and followed him." *The Message.*

It was another beautiful day on the edge of the lake and Jesus was preaching to a growing group of people. He noticed two fishing boats not far from where he was teaching. He saw the owners of the boats and their crews cleaning their nets and tools preparing to put everything away after a long, hard and frustrating night of fishing. Jesus walked by the group, stepped into the boat belonging to Simon (5:3) and continued teaching. The crowd moved with him and gathered around the two groups of tired, smelly, hungry fishermen. A little presumptuous and bold, don't you think?

Jesus didn't know this guy and yet he stepped into the boat and continued preaching after instructing Peter to push him out into the water so that others could hear better. My guess is that Peter would not be in the greatest of moods, here; neither would his coworkers. He was probably thinking to himself, "I'll push you somewhere, all right" because his normal routine, the routine of comfort, and that of his coworkers had been interrupted. They'd busted themselves and sacrificed their entire evening to go out onto the water to fish, like they always did, but got nothing in return. They were tired and just wanted to get things cleaned up so they could go home and have a nice cold one. Then, a crowd gathered around them impeding their efforts.

Yet, just when he's reached the limit of his patience, Jesus finished teaching and Peter walks a little deeper into the murky area of the water to politely pull the boat back towards the beach. Meanwhile, his feet sink deeper and deeper into the wet, mucky mud isolating him between the group of people and Jesus. He stands stuck in a place that will require effort to move regardless of the direction in which he chooses to go and everyone would notice whatever he did next. He's stuck in the quagmire of transition between sacrifice and obedience. He's just stuck. His preference was to stay in sacrifice mode, but Jesus spoke just to him and called him to do something totally offbeat.

He instructed Simon to, "Push out into deep water and let your nets out for a catch" (5:4 *The Message*). This call made no sense to Peter or those watching. He was probably thinking to himself, "you want me to ... *what*?" Jesus called him to use extra effort when he had nothing left in his tank. He was already exhausted. The mere physical cost to pull each leg out of the mud and reorient himself into a position to push the boat out a little further would take everything he had and more. The last thing he wanted to do was push out. The last thing he wanted to do was move himself further into the deeper waters of uncertainty and risk when the safety of the shore was so very appealing.

Simon responded by listing everything that he had done ("we've been fishing hard all night and haven't even caught a minnow" v. 5.) and he could have left it at that, said, "no," and no one would have thought anything less of him. Yet, Jesus offered Simon the opportunity to move from sacrificial stuckitis to experiencing the blessing of obedience. He could stay stuck in the quagmire of "just." Many of us respond to that call with a similar excuse and we just stay stuck in the sacrifice. Everyone watching this would anticipate Peter to stop right after saying the word "minnow" ... but he doesn't.

Simon and Jesus locked gazes and Simon saw that twinkle, maybe even a wink, from Jesus that said, "Come on, you can do this, trust me. I'll give you the strength to push out the boat and watch what's going to happen. Answer my call and watch what happens."

Simon was literally stuck, not just in the sand, but also in the quagmire between sacrifice and obedience. He mentally wrestled in his mind with the excuses: I'm too tired to do anything more. I just want to go home. Why is he looking at me that way? No, just call it a day and get out of here. Why is he calling me to do this? Just call someone else, but that look and his voice. This just makes no sense. Can I trust him? Something's going to happen, here, and I'm going to have to move one way or another cause I can't just stay stuck here. Perhaps all of these thoughts and more raced through Peter's mind until finally he came to terms with the moment of the call and realizes he just can't help himself from wondering what was waiting for him at the other end.

He was going to have to move one leg in front of the other to go home or to join Jesus in the boat. Either way, he was going to have to move and he would remember this moment for the rest of his life. For sure, Simon always looked at that very spot on the beach and remembered that moment. He remembered every time he passed by it and replayed in his mind where Jesus called him to do something out of the ordinary, to really trust him.

What would have happened to Simon if he had ignored Jesus' call or said, "no"? How many times have each of us heard that call and just chosen to ignore it or said "no"?

Perhaps many of us are reminded even to this day of that moment in our lives when we knew God was calling us to do something that made no sense, to trust Him, yet we just chose the safer, more routine option. We settled for boring vanilla rather than the tropicana adventure Jesus has called each of us to.

The Bible records that Simon stepped out in faith. "Master, we've been fishing hard all night and haven't caught even a minnow. But if you say so, I'll let out the nets" (v.5). So, after he and his crew have spent all that time cleaning and trying to put things away, Simon answers the call to undo it all and to cast the nets one more time. Can you imagine the comments of the shore gazers? Shore gazers stay in the "just" mode where they love to make comments about how stupid everyone else looks and how smart they are to be the ones observing from the sidelines, never really putting their faith into action, but always staying "just" safe enough. Shore gazers always forget to factor in the power of the call. The power when Jesus interrupts our daily lives and makes the impossible possible, the ordinary extraordinary, where trust trumps just and our lives are changed forever.

Back to Simon and his crew. Those who obediently answered the call caught so many fish that their nets began to break. That's what happens when we answer the call to step from sacrifice to obedience ... when we trust rather than just ... God confirms the obedience with blessings.[11] Simon and those in his boat experienced a right here ... right now

---

[11] Isaiah 1:19 "If you are willing and obedient, you will eat the best from the land" (NIV).

moment. The other boat went out to help, but only after they had confirmation that something great was happening. Those who gazed upon the happenings from the shore never experienced it firsthand and they missed out on a close encounter with God.

There are always going to be shore gazers, those who are invited, but never get into the boat of obedience. They never really hang out with Jesus experiencing the unexpected and extraordinary. Shore gazers do that. They fear living in the uncertainty of the life that Jesus truly calls each of us to. They just stay stuck in the comfort of protocol and routine and stay off in the distance, influencing as many people as they can to do the same, and sadly never really engage in the adventure. "[F]or many of us the great danger is not that we will renounce our faith ... but settle for a mediocre version of it. We will just skim our lives instead of actually living them."[12]

Each time we answer Jesus' call to push out, we're met with an overwhelming experience that leaves us in awe (v. 9) of what Jesus is able to do and what we're invited to participate in—the Kingdom of God here on earth. "Those who choose to follow Jesus become participants in an insurrection. To claim we believe is simply not enough. The call of Jesus is one that demands action."[13] The opportunities of obedience become so powerful that we respond by offering the only action that we know is right—leaving everything, nets and all (v.11) to follow Him.

[12] John Ortberg, *The Life You've Always Wanted,* (Grand Rapids, MI: Zondervan, 1997), 82.

[13] Erwin Raphael McManus, *The Barbarian Way,* (Nashville, TN: Thomas Nelson Inc, 2005), 5.

I'm convinced that Jesus Christ sits right beside us when we take giant, God-sized risks in answering His call on our lives to trustingly step from sacrifice to obedience. He's waiting with great anticipation that we will answer His call to boldly risk everything and follow His plan for our lives. And, though we may feel overwhelmed at times in our attempts to answer that call and we'll doubt the logistics of it all, feeling like we're going to fall flat on our face if we do, please know, that God is actively guiding us and keeping us from falling down.[14]

Those moments where God has reached into our lives and put new wine into a new wine skin are stories and experiences that He wants us to share with others so that they in turn will step out and risk getting to know Yahweh and let Him work through them to reach others. It's our stories that stand the test of time. Stories of God moving in our lives that get handed down from generation to generation that ensure that we never forget how we have responded to hearing God's voice and how God honored that response, what He has done in us, through us and for us. We remember stories of risk and the resulting life change. They're the ones that become the legend of future generations. Risks that make no sense to those answering the call, and even to those witnessing the response to the call, yet they're boldly pursued as a result of hearing His voice.

God's desire has always been to walk with us. He wants to get rid of whatever we've let into our lives that holds us

---

[14] Psalm 37:24 "Though they stumble, they will never fall, for the LORD holds them by the hand." (NLT).

back and keeps us just stuck from His desires for us. Are we prepared to be honest with ourselves and really open to the opportunity that awaits us when we step from sacrifice to obedience? Where are you in this story? Are you working in the daily routines of life feeling like you're sacrificing a lot and keeping track of everything that you've given up to follow the call? Maybe it's time to erase the ledger, to really trust Him and answer His call to go out a little further and let your nets down. Maybe you know He's calling you, but you're just stuck trying to decide where to go—towards Him or towards the safety of the shore. Maybe you see yourself as a shore gazer never really being part of the story that Jesus invites you into.

Step toward Him so that you can experience the impossible becoming possible. Maybe you're waiting by the other boat for someone else to answer the call and prove that it's safe out on the waters and then you'll respond. Trust the call and pursue it at all costs. The world needs more people to show us how to answer the call. Please know that you can trust Him. He wants you to be like Simon and answer that call from sacrifice to obedience. "Either we wake to tackle our 'to-do' list, get things done ... or we wake in the midst of the dangerous Story, as God's intimate ally, following him into the unknown."[15] Don't you think it's time we truly participated in the story that God wants to write in and through each of us?

---

[15] John Eldredge, *Waking the Dead,* (Nashville, TN: Thomas Nelson Publishers, 2003), 95.

Chapter 9

COST COMPARISON–
SACRIFICE VS. OBEDIENCE

"To be sure, calling is not what it is commonly thought to be.
It has to be dug out from under the rubble of ignorance and
confusion. And, uncomfortably, it often flies directly in the
face of our human inclinations." Os Guinness

"Living the rest of your life for the glory of God will require a
change in your priorities, your schedule, your relationships,
and everything else. It will sometimes mean choosing a
difficult path instead of an easy one." Rick Warren

Our dog has a great personality. She also has the knack for
not doing as I've instructed her to do. This usually happens
at night when just before going to bed I let her outside and
tell her to do her business, not to talk to strangers, skunks,
coyotes, etc., and to quickly return inside for her cookie.
Normally this routine works and when she's done she charges
inside and sits in her bed waiting for the reward for following
the instructions ... the cookie. The operative phrase here is
"normally this routine works." There are times, despite how
many walks she's had that day or the mere fact that we've
provided two square meals for her, that she will at times
totally refuse to answer my call to come inside. She'll stay
just far enough away that we can clearly see each other and

it becomes very obvious that she knows that I know that she knows she's being disobedient. This results in a stare down and then I resort to calling out several times for her to come inside due to the element of stranger danger that could be out there waiting in the bushes. It doesn't work.

This usually happens during really bad weather and I try to explain to her that it's minus 40 and she's going to freeze if she stays out there any longer. That doesn't work, either. Then, as a last ditch effort, I offer, in as nice and sweet a voice as possible, while gritting my teeth, that if she comes in right now she'll get a cookie. That doesn't work, either. I don't get it, but on these evenings when it happens I offer her safety, comfort, protection, and food and she wants none of it, so she stands perfectly still looking at me in complete defiance and disobedience to my instructions even though my instructions are for her own good. Eventually, I just close the door and go about my business for a couple of minutes totally ignoring her. When I go back to check, she's waiting for me at the foot of the door. I open the door and she bounds inside going directly to her bed like nothing had happened and sits and waits for me to give her a cookie.

On those occasions when this doesn't work I call out to Deb and the kids that their dog won't come inside and one of them will come to the door, call her to come inside and the dog immediately bounds inside as if nothing had ever happened and goes to her bed waiting for the cookie.

I don't understand why she doesn't see that I'm calling her to a better situation than the one she's standing in at that time and she never acknowledges all the things I provide for her. Yeah, I know she's just a dog, but she still knows that I know that she knows that I know! After one of these events, she loses her freedom. I take her out on her leash the next time so she can't disobey me. She loses her freedom and it takes a while for her to earn it back. I know she's just a dog, but her disobedience has a definite cost associated to it. It's the same with our relationship with God, especially when He calls us to trust and obey him and we don't. That's definitely sin[1] and it creates a barrier to the relationship continuing and growing to all that God wants and desires it to be.

Consider the Israelites, who had been led by God through Moses out of slavery towards the land God had promised to give them. They'd spent about a year at the base of Mount Sinai preparing for this special journey. They'd all been assigned certain tasks to learn so that collectively they could break camp and follow God's leading toward the Promised Land. This type of operation takes some planning and practice to get all twelve tribes of Israel (around two million people) doing what they're supposed to do, when they're supposed to do it, and in the proper sequence without anyone getting lost or left behind. God would be guiding them toward the new land in the form of a pillar of cloud or fire. Wherever and whenever the presence of God moved, the people picked up camp and obediently followed. They traveled together, worked together at setting up and taking down camp as God guided and directed. Even though God provided for all their needs,

---

[1] Romans 5:19 "For just as through the disobedience of the one man the many were made sinners, so also through the obedience of the one man the many will be made righteous." (NIV).

there were grumblers among them, but the group followed God's call to the Promised Land.[2]

Eventually, they arrived at the edge of the frontier and God called them to pick one representative from each of the tribes of Israel to explore the new land and report back to everyone.[3] Just before the scouts left, Moses instructed them "enter the land boldly"[4] and to bring back some fruit as proof of the beauty of the land. After forty days, the scouts returned and reported that what God has said about the land was true. It was magnificent and beyond their expectations, and they showed some of the fruit they'd found in the land as proof.[5] The grumblers stopped grumbling and the entire two million people were excited about entering the Promised Land, the land promised them as a result of their obedience to following God's call. Then the scouts continued with proverbial, "But ..."[6] and the people turned their focus to the obstacles they'd meet when they entered the new land rather than the blessings that awaited them. They fabricated reasons for not going into the land and very quickly doubt shifted their focus. Only two of the twelve scouts (Caleb and Joshua) stepped forward to try to encourage the Israelites to be obedient and that despite the obstacles before them,

---

[2] Numbers 11:1 "The people soon began to complain to the LORD about their hardships." (NLT).

[3] See Numbers 13:1–2

[4] See Numbers 13:18–20

[5] Numbers 13: 27–28 "We entered the land you sent us to explore, and it is indeed a bountiful country—a land flowing with milk and honey. Here is the kind of fruit it produces. But the people living there are powerful, and their towns are large and fortified. We even saw giants there, the descendants of Anak!" (NLT)

[6] Ibid.

despite the odds, God would deliver!

How short grumblers' memories were. On their journey from Mount Sinai to the borders of Canaan, God lead them through enemy territory without a single altercation. He's shown that no obstacle or person is too big for Him and when people are obedient to answering His call, He will protect them.[7] Yet despite what the Israelites had just experienced on their journey, their doubts multiplied and discouragement set in. Doubt leads us to discouragement which eventually traps us in disobedience. Their focus is on all the reasons why this won't work instead of God's rebuttal of, "Why not let me make it work? Just step out in faith!"

The people's disobedience started with doubt at the logistics of what God was calling them to, which originated from their focus on all the obstacles that stood in the way of where and what God was calling them to do. From there it gathered momentum then spread discouragement amongst the rest of the crowd until the entire group cried out for things to return to the way they used to be. Doubt cast such a large shadow over the camp that the people were even prepared to go back into slavery rather than trusting God to deliver them to freedom.[8] They never did let God take them into the new frontier. The whispers of doubt caused them to drift into disobedience. Despite all the evidence of what God had done

---

[7] Numbers 10: 34–36 "As they moved on each day, the cloud of the Lord hovered over them. And whenever the Ark set out, Moses would shout, 'Arise, O Lord, and let your enemies be scattered! Let them flee before you!' And when the Ark was set down, he would say, 'Return, O Lord, to the countless thousands of Israel!' (NLT).

[8] Numbers 14:4 "Then they plotted among themselves, "Let's choose a new leader and go back to Egypt!" (NLT)

and had been willing to do, they stayed stuck in the past rather than participating in the future blessings from obedience.

Many churches and their leadership are stuck in that very same spot. I witnessed this drifting of doubt and fear recently when a group of church leaders debated what to do about a particular congregation that had drifted by not listening to God. On this particular evening we heard from members of the congregation as to why this was such an unhealthy place, and the two distinct camps within the congregation tried to lobby for support of their interests from the governing body within the denomination, for the umpteenth time I was told, and it was obvious that something radical had to be done. The church was in need of critical care and no one wanted to do what was necessary. It was obvious that the current situation of this congregation and the lack of leadership to step in and do the radical but necessary things required to fix it, had led them once again to this exact quandary.

They had drifted into disobedience and no one was prepared to speak the truth. As the debate continued as to what they should do I felt the Holy Spirit say to me, "Look at their faces and look at their eyes." So as I looked around at all the faces I started to see it—they were all lost in doubt.

Over the many years that this situation had been allowed to continue without being brought back to Godly obedience, doubt had crept in to where it had caused this congregation and the larger group to drift into disobedience. God was nowhere in the equation. Their disobedience had left them in the spiritual desert, aimlessly drifting and calling out for things to be as they used to be and no one was willing to collectively get together that night and ask God for direction. No one was prepared to make the hard decisions and hold people accountable for their disobedience. Everyone had their own interests in not seeking what God wanted to be done.

The need to protect our interests can "discourage us from accepting the high cost of obedience to the truth of the gospel. The pressure to do the most expedient thing is immense, and our minds work overtime trying to find ways to rationalize our disobedience and salve our consciences."[9] This congregation was in serious trouble and they were living in the consequences of their disobedience just like the Israelites were.

The Israelites' disobedience caused an entire generation to miss out on entering the Promised Land and whatever else God had in store for them. For forty years this group wandered the physical and spiritual desert. They weren't totally abandoned by God, but they certainly didn't live up to their God-given potential. So many churches are drifting in disobedience, today, because they've heard God call them to do something and they chose to play it safe. There was a substantial cost to the Israelites' disobedience to God's call[10] just like there is, today. Doubt drifts us into disobedience and lost opportunities to be used by God and blessed by God.

In the case of the Israelites, just one generation later God appointed a new leader for them—Joshua, the same Joshua who was one of only two scouts who tried to get the people to

---

9 David E. Garland, *The NIV Application Commentary, Colossians/Philemon,* (Grand Rapids, MI: Zondervan, 1998), 361.

10 Numbers 14:22 "not one of these people will enter that land. They have seen my glorious presence and the miraculous signs I performed both in Egypt and in the wilderness, but again and again they tested me by refusing to listen" (NLT)

trust God and enter the Promised Land forty years earlier. His willingness to obediently and boldly follow God meant that he and the other scout, Caleb, would be the only two adults from the previous generation of Israelites who would enter the Promised Land. He had never forgotten that moment in history when the people's doubt led them to disobedience which directed the entire group into the desert, and this time he sure wasn't going to see them make the same mistake the previous generation had. He had called the people to trust God back then and never forgot the moment when doubt crept into the camp or the consequences of that doubt.

God chose Joshua to lead the people into the Promised Land and, as God outlines His orders for Joshua to follow, He reminds him of the promises He gave Moses. He tells Joshua that He would be with him, wouldn't leave him hanging out there[11] and encouraged him to be strong and very courageous[12] three separate times all in an effort to hammer home the one point—do not let the people drift into disobedience. Joshua heard God's instructions and he responded with an enthusiastic and excited, "You want me to ... *what?*" He couldn't wait to see what God had in store. He didn't doubt or question or invent excuses. No. He was filled with holy boldness that came from truly believing God's promises and knowing that He'd protect him from failure as long as he didn't let the people drift.

He embraced the role of leadership because he knew that

---

[11] Joshua 1:5 "For I will be with you as I was with Moses. I will not fail you or abandon you" (NLT)

[12] Joshua 1:5,6,7,9

"spiritual leadership is not the ability to define everything the future holds. It is the willingness to move forward when all you know is God."[13] Joshua gathered the people to remind them of the older generation's past mistakes and that they must not turn away from answering God's call into the new frontier. The people followed Joshua and God's direction and faithfully stepped into the Promised Land as a whole nation.

Obedience paid off for them as it led them into the presence of God.[14] Their faithful response to answering God's call eliminated all the obstacles that the previous generation saw as too great to overcome. Their obedience prompted God to walk ahead and eliminate all of the obstacles and doubts that could cause them to drift. Their obedient, faithful response to God's call to do something that required great focus and trust was rewarded. Because they did not drift into disobedience as their parents had, they witnessed God moving in their lives. His presence surrounded the whole group, obliterated the obstacles and enemies in their lives. This generation corrected the drifting by the previous generation. They wrote a new story for the next generation to talk about and the same is true for us, today.

Our reaction to God's call to enter new frontiers has a tremendous impact on the next generation and how they in turn pursue God. They're watching us and noticing our level of obedience/disobedience and whether or not the presence of God is truly moving amongst us. This is a key element to

---

[13] Erwin Raphael McManus, *An Unstoppable Force — Daring to Become the Church GOD had in Mind,* (Loveland, CO: Group Publishing Inc., 2001), 77.

[14] Joshua 3:10 "Today you will know that the living God is among you" (NLT)

gauging how effective our church communities are, as well.

Many congregations are dying. And those congregations are usually marked by the spiritual pride of wanting the glory days to come back. A little turmoil and gossip and they're stuck in the spiritual desert. It's not like God hasn't been calling them to step out. He has, it's just that they've ignored that call and drifted, aimlessly, into the spiritual desert caused by disobedience. These churches have trusted more in the way they want things to stay and so they've retreated to living a life like a patient on their death bed just waiting for the heart to stop beating so they can die. You know the saying "I'm all for change, but do it once I'm dead." These congregations are affecting everyone in their community, and the sad thing is that if you asked those in the surrounding community who are not attending any church at all if they'd miss that particular church if it closed its doors the answer would be a unanimous, "No!"

Similarly, every congregation has a small, but vocal group of long-standing believers who sit and criticize any new initiatives in the worship services or ministry venues that might appeal in a fresh way to the unreached in the community. Every congregation has them, their complaints fuelled by their focus on the glory days. "If we disobey God's will (whether in outright defiance or more subtle neglect), the consequences are an unhealthy church with messed-up priorities."[15]

How about the believer who feels that God only moves in a specific, well-defined, neat, orderly, and according to

---

[15] Neil Cole, *Organic Church—Growing Faith Where Life Happens,* (San Francisco, CA: Jossey-Bass, 2005), 42.

their perspective of how things should be done way? The neat, clean, orderly one is usually the first to speak out against the suggestion of stepping out to answer God's call by discounting the validity of the call itself because the call is to do something completely "unconventional" and outside of their understanding of how God calls. These types of complainers existed in Moses' and Joshua's days and they exist in our churches, today. They're shore gazers who have gradually and very subtly drifted into disobedience and their primary purpose is to stay in comfortable survival mode while influencing as many within the tribe as possible to do the same. They drift in the comfort of doubt and attempt to dissuade. If you follow them or let them influence you they'll cause you to drift into disobedience where you'll miss God's direction and the blessing He has in store for your obedience.

Perhaps their lack of faithful trust in stepping out for God is rooted somewhere in their past where they saw the previous generation continually ignore God's call or justify with some lame excuse as to why they shouldn't answer God's call to do a brand new thing.[16] If their past experience had been one where the previous generation had run full out toward God by answering His call, giving everything they had to boldly see where God would call them, then maybe their reaction to God doing something brand new would be more enthusiastic. Instead of criticizing and casting doubt they'd be leading the charge to experience the powerful

---

[16] Isaiah 43:18,19 "Forget about what's happened; don't keep going over old history. Be alert, be present. I'm about to do something brand-new. It's bursting out! Don't you see it? There it is! I'm making a road through the desert, rivers in the badlands." *The Message.*

presence of God working through them and influencing others to do the same thing. Playing it safe and drifting in comfort isn't biblical.

I don't know about you, but playing it safe is not the message I want to leave my kids or grandkids. I want them to see firsthand how God has followed through on His promise to use me when I step out in faith and to remove the obstacles and enemies that stand before me when I'm following God's call to obedience full out. Who knows, perhaps "more people would find the Christian community more interesting if we were the ones having a wild time instead of cringing at the thought of having a wild time."[17]

Our desire to be obedient to God's call is a journey on the road called life. It's a relational road with God, full of twists, turns and destinations along the way to a better understanding of God, us and who He calls us to be *right here ... right now*. "God doesn't owe you an explanation or reason for everything he asks you to do. Understanding can wait, but obedience can't. Instant obedience will teach you more about God than a lifetime of Bible discussions. In fact, you will never understand some commands until you obey them first. Obedience unlocks understanding."[18] Our obedience will take us places we'd never expect to be in and events that we would have never written for ourselves. However, if we're to fully engage the road God wants us to travel on and explore in this life then we must learn to read

---

[17] Rick Bundschuh, *Don't Rock the Boat Capsize It — Loving the Church Too Much to Leave It the Way It Is,* (Colorado Springs, CO: NavPress, 2005), 89.

[18] Warren, *The Purpose Driven Life,* 72.

the road signs along the way and obediently follow His road signs, trusting that He knows the way better than we do. This is where God wants us to be and where He does some of His greatest lessons for us to gain deeper understanding.

Sometimes God makes it very clear where we're to go and how we're to get there. Long before the Israelites entered the Promised Land, God led them out of the land of Egypt where they had been slaves (Exodus 14:5–25). On their left was the advancing band of ticked-off Egyptians and on their right was a giant body of water (the Red Sea). With nowhere else to go, the Israelites complained and wished they were back in Egypt. Fear had frozen the people from doing anything. Moses told them to not be afraid as God would do everything and they wouldn't have to lift a finger.[19] (I wonder how many really believed that and broke out in cheering and clapping? I'm sure not many.) Then God told Moses to lift his hand over the water[20] and He would do the rest.

God created a wall between the Israelites and the Egyptians with His presence, making it very obvious where the Israelites needed to go. The only option available required Moses to follow God's instruction and raise his hand over the water. That's it ... nothing more nothing less. Follow His way and God will do the rest.

---

[19] Exodus 14:13 "But Moses told the people, "Don't be afraid. Just stand still and watch the Lord rescue you today. The Egyptians you see today will never be seen again." (NLT)

[20] Exodus 14:16, 21, 22 "Raise your staff and stretch out your hand over the sea to divide the water so that the Israelites can go through the sea on dry ground. Then Moses stretched out his hand over the sea, and all that night the Lord drove the sea back with a strong east wind and turned it into dry land. The waters were divided, and the Israelites went through the sea on dry ground, with a wall of water on their right and on their left." (NIV).

Allow me to paraphrase. God said to Moses, "Look, if we're going to really work together, here, I need some participation from you. So, I'll tell you what I need you to do and I'll even tell you everything I'm going to do in advance leaving nothing to doubt. I'll make it very obvious that the only thing you have to do is the simple act of raising your hand. No one will notice, but I want you to experience a different level of obedience so that you can see what I'm willing to do for those who answer my call." God didn't tell Moses to do something really radical. All he had to do was raise one hand in obedience and God would move in ways they'd never seen before. "Be obedient and watch my blessing!" There are times when God will move first to make it very clear as to where He wants us to go, just like He did for our family when we answered the call to move to Windsor. God made it very clear that He was calling us to move to a new land.

Once we're on this new path, it's not long before we come to a curve in the road and God calls us toward a new direction, toward a God-ordained situation that will enhance and deepen our understanding of obedience. One such example is in the continuation of the story from the book of Joshua discussed earlier in this chapter. One generation from the experience at the Red Sea, God told Joshua to cross the Jordan River and enter the Promised Land. God told Joshua to take twelve men, one from each tribe of Israel, to carry the Ark of the Covenant and have them step into the waters of the river first and only then would He act by stopping the rivers upstream from flowing so that the people will be able to cross the river as one nation.[21] The Ark symbolized to the people of Israel that God's presence and power was with them and as the people walked with God it was their step of faith into the river that showed their trusting obedience to God's call to a new direction.

Once they stepped into the waters that divided the old from the new, the mistakes of disobedience from the previous generation from a new way, toward a new land full of God's promise, God stopped the water and showed them where to walk. They stepped out in faith, first, then God delivered what He had in store for them. They heard God's call, but it would first require their action ... a step of faith ... into the unknown waters.

Each respective body of water (Red Sea and Jordan River) separated God's people from a new frontier and direction He was calling them to. Both accounts are right here ... right now moments in the history of the Israelites. Steps of faith taken in obedience led them to experience great acts of God's power and a much deeper understanding of what obedience entails. The key difference in these two stories is our understanding that sometimes God speaks and moves first to make it very obvious what we're to do (like Moses and the Israelites), and other times God tells us what we need to do and what He'll do only after we act by stepping out in faith. Have you had situations like these in your own life?

---

[21] Joshua 3:8, 13 "Give this command to the priests who carry the Ark of the Covenant: 'When you reach the banks of the Jordan River, take a few steps into the river and stop there ... The priests will carry the Ark of the Lord, the Lord of all the earth. As soon as their feet touch the water, the flow of water will be cut off upstream, and the river will stand up like a wall." (NLT).

This type of situation happened for me and my family. It wasn't long into the New Year when both Deb and I sensed that God was trying to get our attention. By the end of November, God had brought a buyer for our previous home, which freed us up to move from renting the Pastor's Palace to purchasing a new home. We felt that if this was where God was calling us to be then we should really put down roots in this community by having a house built for us, even though my real estate background (human logic) said to continue renting. We lifted it up in prayer asking for God to close this door if we weren't to purchase a home, here. We ended up building a beautiful home and the normal routine of daily life was moving along just fine. Just fine, that is, until we got a phone call letting us know that a good friend of ours back in Barrie had been in a terrible car accident and she'd been rushed to the critical care unit in a Toronto hospital. They didn't think that she would make it through the night. Both Deb and I felt a strong prompting to go that night to the hospital so we packed up the van and began the four-hour trip to the hospital.

I knew that our visit wasn't to be a social one. As nice as it was going to be to see all our old friends, we weren't going to get involved in all the "stuff" going on at our old church. No, I really felt that God was directing me to get in to see her, to pray over her and anoint her with oil. So that night we left for the hospital and as we walked into the critical care floor we were met with a sea of people, all of whom were praying for her healing. After a while God created the opportunity for me to get in to see her and pray over her. Such an opportunity for a pastor is one that is on sacred ground. It was amazing to get close to her and pray what the Holy Spirit was directing, anointing her with oil; and as I closed my eyes and lay my hands on her head I was met with a vision of a large angel with huge wings standing at the head of the bed with its hand on her shoulders. What a comforting and hopeful visual for the worst and probably most hopeless floor in any hospital. I'm glad to say that God answered the thousands of prayers that were lifted for her as she is currently walking down the road of recovery.

A couple of days later, we returned to Windsor and resumed our daily routine at least to the best of our abilities, but both Deb and I realized that something had happened at the hospital. We both felt a strong pull to this group of people, but we just weren't sure of its meaning. Both of us knew that things were different, not really sure how it was different, just that it was. God had used that situation to get our attention, stir our spirits, and over the next several weeks and months that stirring grew.

Deb and I discussed with each other the many things we had become aware of and were trying to make sense of it in our hearts. It had become very obvious that we needed to be as one in prayer and devotion time if we were to discern what God was trying to say. So Deb and I began to read the same scripture readings each day, and after we had our own quiet reflection time we would talk about the things that God had brought to our attention through His word and what He was laying on our hearts. It became very apparent that the Holy Spirit was starting to lay an identical foundational message in our devotion time and the message was that things were going to change. God's message of doing a brand new thing and the theme of going back home was repeated for months in our daily readings and confirmed in our reflective prayer time.

God moved in many different ways. Deb's maternity/ long-term occasional position would run out at the end of the 2008 school year. We thought for sure that this would be her chance to get her foot in the door in a school because she had shown the administration that she was worth hiring on a full-time basis. In the meantime, she was busy tracking down any lead to get a contract position within the Board of Education in Windsor. She applied for a special position with the guidance arm of the board and one for which she was very well qualified. Deb invested a huge amount of time researching and preparing for the interview so she would "wow" them and stand a good chance of being offered the job. Then, on the morning of the interview just before 7:00 a.m. our phone rang and the caller asked to speak to Deb.

It was the Superintendent of the Board. He said that he was really impressed with her qualifications and he was sure that she was more than qualified to do the job and she'd probably do a phenomenal job for them, but they couldn't interview her for the position because she hadn't been hired on a full-time basis within the board. She was crushed, but kept her composure and asked that if they didn't find a suitable candidate in this go around that she be reconsidered at that time. He replied "no" since in essence she was on the outside of the board, and even though she could be the very best qualified person to do the job, she would not be considered for the job. This was a continuation of God speaking and getting our attention.

Then we got another sign. When we moved down to Windsor, Deb had taken a leave of absence from the teaching board where she had a full-time contract. We discussed the options available to us prior to moving down to Windsor and due to the pension fund and benefits it made sense to apply for a leave of absence until she was able to get a full-time teaching job in Windsor. We thought that a two-year leave would be plenty of time for her to get in full-time in the Windsor Board and once that had been coordinated she would transfer her position from one board to another. When she applied for the original leave, she was told that the leave would be given in two one-year terms with the second term of the leave being just a formality and by Spring of 2008 she would be required to just send in the request for the extended leave term of one more year and it would be granted. When Deb requested the extended leave, she was told that it would not be granted. We can plan all we want, but if God wants to do a brand new thing in our lives His way is not the same as ours.

On top of that, at her review with the principal at the school where she was teaching in Windsor she was told that the teaching prospects in the Windsor board were becoming very slim and even though she was a great teacher, and she would love to hire her, the reality was there were no new hires planned anywhere in the board for at least the next five to seven years. Then it was announced that almost one hundred full-time teachers would be shifted to the supply list within the board and all of these teachers would be competing for any supply/long-term occasional positions that would come up in the fall of 2008. God was getting our attention. Deb was fully prepared to leave her position back home if God wanted us to stay as both our hearts were beating with the desire to be obedient to God's call wherever that was. Oftentimes God uses the daily events of our lives to reflect and confirm the message of His word.

The job at Lakeshore was going well and I continued to learn so much from so many gifted people. Attendance was increasing, people were surrendering their lives to Jesus Christ, lives were being transformed and the community was being affected by our presence. We did a series about what it would look like if we could see God's dreams for us, and it was during one of the messages in this series that God spoke to me, adding another layer of indication that He was preparing my heart for something brand new.

One day, after hosting a function in the church, the staff was busy cleaning up and putting away the tables, chairs, and everything else. I started vacuuming the room. I was alone and in the middle of taking a corner where the dust bunnies were running in fear. The vacuum was whirring like a sleek-designed racing car, and that voice spoke, again, saying, "It's time to write it." I heard it, but not wanting to lose any momentum with the vacuum I keep vacuuming, knowing full well that if I stopped and spoke out loud "what do you mean?" it would be the precise time that someone would walk around the corner and hear me talking out loud to the vacuum.

God had laid on my heart a couple of different themes to expand on in book form (of which this is the first) and while I hadn't done anything about it, yet, it was becoming obvious that

He wanted me to get going on that front. God was activating the hidden conduits of a spirit-filled awakening within me to charge me to get going on it and to do something I'd never done before: write. I heard the voice and acknowledged that I'd heard Him speak and it lined up with the rest of the events unfolding in our family life. "God chooses us, gives us grace, and redeems the story of our lives. That is ultimately his will for us. Only then does he call us to do his will in the ordinariness of life."[22] And so, in the middle of vacuuming, I heard Him call and I knew something new awaited me.

That same week, during one of Lakeshore St. Andrew's elders meetings, our Senior Pastor announced that one of our session members was going to be leaving the area and the church. He said that he and his family would definitely be missed and expressed his appreciation that this couple had invited him and his wife into the discernment process early on so that they could walk with this family during such a time and would not be blindsided by their announcement and decision to leave without any consultation. I saw this as a sign for me to do the same thing and so Deb and I met with my boss and his wife to let them know that we felt like God was doing something and He might be calling us to move back. This was a great time to open the dialogue and have them speak into the situation while lifting it up in prayer. Needless to say they were surprised, didn't think that it made sense, but appreciated being involved early on so that they could begin to pray. They made it clear that while they didn't

---

[22] Jerry Sittser, *The Will of God as a Way of Life,* (Grand Rapids, MI: Zondervan, 2004), 105.

feel like God was calling us away they wanted us to be where God wanted us to be. Perhaps God uses surprises to jolt us out of the routine of comfort so we're forced to draw closer to Him and rely on His grace in those moments when we begin to stretch ourselves, expand the boundaries of our tent, move its pegs and change our comfort zone.[23]

One Sunday in January 2008, a very dynamic and powerful guest preacher visited our church. As I learned more about his story I was blown away by the message of it all. He went from being the Associate Pastor in a mega-church in the Chicago area, where everyone thought he was the heir apparent to replace the Senior Pastor when he retired, to responding to God's call for him to enter a new frontier of planting a church in downtown Detroit. It made no sense whatsoever except for the God factor and his stepping out in faith to answer God's call. Even to this day there are people at his previous church who feel he made a mistake, and yet the people in his current flock would strongly disagree. God was speaking to me through this story.

Answering the call took him out of the routine of the expected and into the midst of God's presence in a new way. This was a new direction along the journey of life that he hadn't expected or experienced before. Right here ... right now moments do that to the routines of our lives. It was obvious to me that God had called this particular individual to do something brand new that to some made no sense whatsoever. But to God, it made all the sense in His world because of the

---

[23] Isaiah 54:2 "Enlarge the place of your tent, stretch out your curtains wide, do not hold back" (NIV).

story He wanted to write in this gentleman's life.

I sought additional guidance from some of my spiritual mentors and discussed with them the concept behind what we thought God was doing. All of them affirmed that oftentimes God will call us to do the unexpected and to step out of the comfort of the daily routine by doing something that makes no sense. However, it is the discerning part where God stretches us by putting new wine into new wine skins that is difficult. Discerning takes time, and both Deb and I were sure that if God were calling us to go, we didn't want to rush into anything that wasn't God ordained and directed.

In one of my conversations, a friend shared with me his own recent situation where God had called him to leave a successful ministry. He hadn't gone looking for something new, but God used a situation to prompt his heart to test its openness to the concept of God's call to leave his current ministry. The idea itself caught him totally off guard. He then shared how sometimes God uses the initial prompting to get our attention and yet His plan has something totally different in mind from the original prompting. His situation held true to that observation as he confirmed with the Word, through time in prayer and conversations with his own group of spiritual advisors. It became obvious that God was calling him to a totally different congregation than he had ever even considered. That's so God.

I listened to all these conversations. We stayed focused in the Word and prayed very hard. There wasn't a panic to it, but a peaceful curiosity of pursuing God's direction here and trusting that He will look after all of the details and the timing for everything to happen if in fact He had called us to do something.

I shared the situation with another mentor and talked about the different fleeces that we'd put out to get a sense of God's direction. We'd used fleeces before to better understand God's direction, and so as part of discerning we put a couple more to see what would happen. I shared how nothing seemed to be happening with these fleeces, which added another level to the whole discerning part of the equation. It was in this conversation that the mentor said that fleeces work at the early stages of people learning to walk with and respond to God's leading, but if we're to grow in our spiritual life with God, it's His desire to have us hear Him speak and to obediently respond in faith without introducing fleeces of any kind.

Gideon was the one who used the fleece concept.[24] God approached Gideon and called him a mighty warrior.

"Are you talking to me?" Gideon responded. "I'm the weakest of the weak and the smallest of the small and I have no social ranking whatsoever and you, God, greet me by calling me a mighty warrior. I don't believe that it's actually you God, so give me a sign to know that it's you."[25]

God sent down fire to consume a meal offering that Gideon had placed on a rock. Once God had Gideon's attention, he instructed Gideon to cause some trouble in the village by taking down some altars that the people had built to another god. Gideon heard God's instruction, but carried

---

[24] Judges 6, 7

[25] Judges 6:12–18

it out at night so as to not be seen by his family and friends.[26] Then God gave Gideon a larger task to complete, which was to lead the people into a major battle. Gideon looked for assurance from God even though God had already been proven trustworthy. Nonetheless, Gideon put two more fleeces out there and God responded to those fleeces. After that, God spoke to Gideon audibly[27] and Gideon never put another fleece out. He just responded when he heard God call him to do something. He put his faith into action and God used him and the small group of warriors to trounce a much larger enemy.

Gideon's relationship with God grew stronger each time he responded to God's call. What started as placing fleeces for assurance that God would follow through, shifted into a greater ability to hear the voice of God and respond to His leading by stepping out and following in faith. My mentor felt that this was what God was trying to teach us in this process of discerning God's direction for us and that's why the fleeces we had placed weren't being answered. He was stretching us out of the comforts of our previous routines and, like Gideon, God was teaching us to hear His voice and gain a deeper understanding of His call to a new land.

My mentor said that God probably wouldn't answer the fleeces as I expected, but would only answer them, like Abraham, after I stepped out in faith.[28] When God

---

[26] Judges 6:27

[27] Judges 7:2,4,5,7,9

[28] Genesis 12:1 "The LORD had said to Abram, "Leave your country, your people and your father's household and go to the land I will show you." (NIV).

called Abraham, he was seventy-five years old and living a comfortable life. Yet he responded to God's call even though he didn't know where he or his family were going.

There was a moment in that conversation that I didn't want to deal with and that was the potential that God was growing us in our faith and fine tuning our ways of hearing His calling. Part of this learning for me was the whole concept of really stepping out and being obedient to God's call without knowing what was next. That made me uncomfortable because it meant that I would be putting my faith into action to a larger and deeper level than ever before.

So, what does it look like when God starts to speak and reveal His direction for our lives? I don't know if there's one complete answer to that. What I do know is He speaks to each of us in different ways, ways that stir our spirit. That is of course if we're really listening for God's voice and desiring to hear His call. His call stirs our spirit because He's the one who made us, knows us better than anyone, and knows how to get our attention in ways that resonate with us.[29] And, all the promptings and stirrings will line up with and be confirmed by His word. I have found that God does repeatedly bring things to our attention especially at times when we are trying to discern His will for our lives.

During this time of discernment, one of my spiritual mentors asked me how things were coming along in the understanding of what God was trying to say to me. I started to explain how I just wanted Him to hit me over the head

---

[29] Psalm 139:13 "You created my inmost being; you knit me together in my mother's womb." (NIV).

with a two-by-four and make it really obvious as to what the next step was to be. I was told to relax.

"You'll know when you know."

I didn't understand that point, then. One hour later my Senior Pastor popped into my office to ask how things were coming along with the discerning process and whether we'd had any further inclinations or revelations about what God was up to. I said that we were still working through it and his response was—you guessed it, "Just relax. You'll know when you know."

To hear the exact same phrase from two godly people was a little God nudge for me that affirmed that He was right there in the middle of it walking with me.

If our heart's intent is to bring honor to God in everything we do and to love Him with everything we have, then when we put our faith into action, even if we make the wrong decisions or bungle up the whole process of discerning, it's okay. God will redirect us and bring us back to where He wants us to be. He wants more people to step out in faith rather than staying stuck in the routine of comfort.

That advice helped me a great deal and hopefully it will help you as you press in to hear God's voice and as you discern the direction of His call and the cost of answering that call. "When God communicates with us, and we respond to Him, our relationship becomes deeper and more meaningful"[30] and this is only achieved by our constant desire and repeated attempts to hear God's call and obediently respond in action. What is He

---

[30] Chuck D. Pierce, Rebecca Wagner Systema, *When God Speaks,* (Ventura, CA: Regal Books, 2005), 33.

calling you to do, now? Are you willing to lay down the excuses and act? Now is the time ... *right here ... right now.*

Chapter 10

DEEPER THAN OBEDIENCE—
GIVING GOD THE PEN

"Twenty years from now you will be more disappointed
by the things that you didn't do than by the ones
you did do. So throw off the bowlines. Sail away from
the safe harbor. Catch the trade winds in your sails.
Explore. Dream. Discover." Mark Twain

"God has chosen to link Himself with us in the
accomplishment of His eternal purposes. He uses us to make
a difference in the world ... God gives us the opportunity to
be difference-makers *for our blessing.*" Don Cousins

"If we live by the [Holy] Spirit, let us also walk by the Spirit. [If
by the Holy Spirit we have our life in God, let us go forward
walking in line, our conduct controlled by the Spirit.]"
Galatians 5:25 (AMP)

One of the many things I love about God is that so often when
I get the opportunity to share His word with people, people
who have gathered expecting to hear a message from God
that directly relates to their own individual lives, He never
disappoints. Oftentimes, the message He puts on my heart to
share with others is usually one that applies directly to me,
first. It will be something He wants to draw my attention to
in my own life and so the message wrestles with me before
reaching others. In this way, God reveals His sense of humor

and never ending desire to reach into our lives and teach us the truth of His way[1] and that way is full of right here ... right now moments.

God's story for my life took another step toward clarity while I was preparing two sermons I was to give on back-to-back Sundays. They were part of a series that Lakeshore St. Andrew's was doing on dreams. It covered a wide net and dealt with such things as the dreams we have for our lives, how God answers dreams, and why dreams go unanswered, etc. It was a powerful kick off to start the New Year and, once again, God shook me deep inside of my core during this series.

Earlier in this book, I talked about my dream of owning a golf course, and then giving it up. At this moment in my life, I was uncovering a new dream that God had planted within me in the last couple of years and one that I had only shared with my wife. Who knows how long it had lain there dormant? On those two Sundays, I knew God opened my eyes and shifted my focus to look at and hear the beating of my heart and what had started to stir within me as a result of preaching God's word.

The messages were inspired from a parable written by Bruce Wilkinson called "The Dream Giver." It's a wonderful story about a character named Ordinary who was a Nobody living in the land of Familiar. "[F]or the most part not much happened in Familiar that hadn't happened before. He found the routines reliable. He blended in with the crowd. And mostly, he wanted only what he had. Until one day Ordinary

---

[1]   Psalm 86:11 "Teach me your ways, O LORD,that I may live according to your truth! Grant me purity of heart, so that I may honor you." (NLT).

noticed a small, nagging feeling that something was missing from his life. Or maybe the feeling was that *he* was missing from something big. He wasn't sure. The little feeling grew. And even though Nobodies in Familiar didn't generally expect the unexpected, Ordinary began to wish for it."[2] He hears and sees clues left for him by the dream giver (God) and so Ordinary sets out on a journey to find what God was calling him to pursue and the result changes his life and those around him forever. He uncovers this big dream within him and struggles through all the obstacles in his way. As he does so it becomes clear that God has such a dream for everyone in the town of Familiar. This story spoke to me on so many levels and I couldn't let go of the question, "What would it look like if we sought God's dream for our lives?" Does God have a dream for each of us? Does he have more than one?

Dreams are powerful catalysts that God uses to move us toward something far bigger than the limits we place on possibilities. That is, for the very few who dare to chase them. We find great motivation in watching others chase those dreams because somewhere in the recesses of our souls we find it easier to watch others and live vicariously through their efforts than to expend the effort of seeking our own. Sadly, we celebrate the others' journeys while embracing the safety of our couches.

The greatest television audience tunes in every two years to watch the Olympics. At no other time in the daily life of our planet do so many people gather in one common focus of

---

2   Bruce Wilkinson, *The Dream Giver,* (Sisters, OR: Multnomah Publishing, 2003), 13–14.

watching and celebrating the stories of people who have sought and dared to risk going after a dream that was planted in their soul's years before. We love those stories. Why? It's the heartbeat of being human where we're stirred to push past obstacles and achieve something bigger than ourselves. It's inside each of us and God has placed it there. We long to participate in something that is far greater than ourselves because just like Ordinary, God had planted something in each of us. "Deep in our hearts, we all want to find and fulfill a purpose bigger than ourselves. Only such a larger purpose can inspire us to heights we know we could never reach on our own."[3]

Recently, a group of students from Humber College in Toronto did just that. They gathered together to reach a common goal by achieving something that many thought impossible—they contacted the International Space Station. The odds were stacked against them and the obstacles that they had to overcome just to make the attempt at reaching their dream were piled high. If they were to make contact with the Space Station, they would have to transmit over a distance of approximately 370 miles, or 600 kilometers, without any interference, hook up with a target that was traveling at a speed of over 16,700 miles per hour, or 27,000 kilometers per hour, and do it within a ten-minute window. They did it using a radio system that they designed from scratch using normal everyday radio materials. No one had ever done this before and they were constantly criticized by their peers and told that it was crazy and would never work. Yet, they had this collective dream that inspired them to work

---

[3] Guinness, *The Call*, 3.

together to achieve what many in their town of Familiar said was impossible. They successfully accomplished their dream despite all the obstacles, criticisms, doubters, shore gazers and drifters that stood around and watched this group of people get off the couch and do something that no one had ever achieved before.

How powerful would our witness be to the world if every Christian in the world decided that they were going to respond to God's dream for their lives, today, to put their faith into action despite the obstacles and criticisms they would face with that decision? If "our faith is going to be criticized, let it be for the right reasons. Not because we are too emotional, but because we're not emotional enough; not because our passions are so powerful, but because they are so puny; not because we are too affectionate, but because we lack a deep, passionate, uncompromising affection for Jesus Christ."[4] What if more of us decided to be like those students and let our faith be criticized because we have followed the call of Jesus Christ with reckless pursuit and done so because His call stirs the core of our heart to respond. Our response should not be one of excuses as to why we shouldn't do something or why it doesn't make sense or why it won't work, but rather our response should be founded in asking ourselves, why not? Why not chase the dream that God has waiting for you and me? Why not follow the leading and call of our Lord to a fully trusting, obedient, and passionate life that can impact and influence those around us to do the same

---

[4] Brennan Manning, *The Ragamuffin Gospel,* (Sisters, OR: Multnomah Publishers, 2000), 162.

thing? After all, didn't Jesus do the same for us?

One of the students attending the event as a spectator won the chance to ask astronaut Sandra Magnus the following question: "Many people have given up hope because they cannot see what's beyond them. What do you say to anyone whose eyes have not beheld the vast wonders of the world you've seen?" Magnus replied that she saw the world from a different viewpoint and she saw it not as groups of individuals (people or countries), but rather that "we're one huge group of people and we're all in this together."[5]

What would our own lives look like if we shifted our viewpoint and tried to the best of our abilities to see things the way that God sees our lives? What would it look like if our perspective changed and we saw the potential that awaits each of us and the dreams He has for us? What would it look like if we only had the strength and courage to leave the land of Familiar and pursue the dream He has placed inside each of us? Don't you think that God's perspective of how things look and what awaits us is far greater than what we could imagine on our own? It's got to be, because we're made in His image[6] and so part of Him is inside us, including His great plans and dreams for us.

Back in the land of Familiar, the stirring of Ordinary's soul is growing and he knows that there's more to his life than what he has. One day he's at his parents' house and he

---

[5] Cynthia Reason, Humber's Operation First Contact a success after students talk to astronaut, Etobicoke Guardian, February 3, 2009, (http:www// insidetoronto.com/Article/63187, accessed on March 3, 2009).

[6] Genesis 1:27 "So God created man in his own image, in the image of God he created him; male and female he created them." (NIV)

shares this stirring of his soul with his dad and how he feels like he's called to be a Somebody who achieves great things in his life. His dad confirms that Ordinary is on to something and then shares the story of how he, too, had a dream, but he kept putting it off until eventually it was gone never to appear again. He tells Ordinary not to make the same mistake that he did. One can't fail in any attempt at doing something. Our greatest failure comes when we don't do anything at all.[7]

Every single one of us will encounter the moment when we realize that our time on earth has an end. It's the symbol that sits at the end of the written and unwritten elements that comprise the story of our lives. This moment is magnified when we witness the stages of death just before someone takes their last breath. Death has a way of dealing with the unspoken realities of those things in our lives that we have put off doing. It rips away the mask of pride and exposes the parts of life that we would give anything to change at that moment, but by then it's too late. If people on their death beds would talk about their deep thoughts as they stare death in the face, most will admit that deep down inside they regret never following the dream that they've ignored or kept buried deep inside of them. They may not acknowledge who placed the dream inside of them, but if you ask they'll open up and discuss what parts of their lives they would do differently and how they wished they'd had more courage to tackle the fears that held them back from exploring the unexplored recesses of their dreams.

Courage is our sledgehammer. We use it as an instrument

---

[7] Manning, *The Ragamuffin Gospel,* 170.

to dismantle the walls of fear in our lives. At the root of courage is heart and it's our heart that either keeps us focused on God's will for our lives (His dreams for us) or distracts us with the familiar and routine so we miss being in sync with God's heartbeat for us.[8]

As I prepared to share with the congregation the messages that God had laid on my heart, He was also making me keenly aware that He was calling me to something outside of the land of Familiar. I didn't want to make the mistake of missing the moment, the moment where my heart beat in sync with God's heart. So, while I pushed and completed my preparation to deliver these messages, God was prepping me for another right here ... right now moment. He was opening my eyes to the dream He wanted to write, a story, a letter if you will, that would get my attention. Letters are great reminders of places we wanted to go, things we wanted to accomplish and places where we ended up. They're a snapshot of a memory and moment in time. They force us to look at the snapshot of our lives in a three-dimensional past, present, and future perspective. They give us a chance to rewrite our future based on our honest reflection of the moments we've missed along the journey.

By total fluke early one summer, good friends were visiting and we began to talk about spending New Years together even though it was a good many months away. Somewhere in the conversation we thought that it would be great to have all of

---

[8] Acts 13:22 "After Saul had ruled forty years, God removed him from office and put King David in his place, with this commendation: 'I've searched the land and found this David, son of Jesse. He's a man whose heart beats to my heart, a man who will do what I tell him." *The Message.*

us write down on a piece of paper our dreams for the next year so everyone wrote theirs down on the piece of paper without looking at anyone else's and then we sealed it in an envelope, putting it away until New Year's Eve. It was hilarious to read these out loud the following year and the whole thing was so insightful that we made it a tradition.

In the beginning none of my dreams and aspirations had anything to do with God, church, school, Windsor, etc. Things don't always go the way you plan them to and even though our dreams could be good ones, oftentimes we forget to factor in God's guiding influence and desire to participate in our lives. Over the years these letters have revealed a trend of transition for my own journey where I moved from no desire for God, to being able to show Him how much I'd given up for him, to writing of my uncertainty of what lay ahead for the upcoming year, and my desire that whatever it was that it would be pleasing to Him. The shift in the focus of my dreams and desires over those years was similar to the shift we're called to in the Christian journey.

What would it look like if God wrote a similar letter for each of us each year with each letter forming a chapter in the story of our lives? It would be spectacular for sure!

Do you think God's dream for each of us is bigger, equal to, or smaller than the dreams we dream for ourselves? Would we write huge God-sized dreams if our perspective changed so that we could see things the way God sees things? Probably. If we're to leave the Land of Familiar and to pursue the dream that God wants to write in and through us, we will need to let go of the pen, give it to God and let Him write it. We must have a heart like David and a willingness to do what God tells us to do whenever He tells us to do it. It means that we must surrender our insecurities, fears, doubts, the good opinions of others, lack of resources, or a clear cut map, and whatever else holds us back from experiencing what God is waiting to write for us. It means that we must move into a different level of obedience, one of surrender, and it starts by releasing the pen we're using to write the stories of our lives. We must risk letting go of the pen and giving it over to God.

A recent University study on risk and its effect on people's lives proved that people who are willing to take risks live more satisfying lives, and parents who are more willing to take risks have children who are more prepared to take risks. Perhaps they're more open to hearing the call to leave the Land of Familiar and pursue something out of the ordinary.[9]

God's dream for us isn't about playing it safe or staying stagnant and comfortable. No, His dreams for us are not super-sized. They're God-sized. They're beyond our ability to comprehend and they need to be that big so that there's enough room for Him to participate with us in the dream. He wants to write Himself into the story of our lives, that's the whole essence of the Bible, and include Himself in His dreams that await us. But first, we must surrender the pen

---

[9] "Success A Family Affair? Willingness to Take Risks and Trust Others Are Inherited, Study Suggests," *ScienceDaily* University of Bonn (November 29, 2006). Retrieved February 22, 2009, from http://www.sciencedaily.com/releases/2006/11/061128140652.htm and "No Risk, No Fun? People Who Take Risks More Satisfied With Their Lives," *ScienceDaily,* University of Bonn (September 19, 2005). Retrieved February 22, 2009, from http://www.sciencedaily.com/releases/2005/09/050919081143.htm.

that writes the story of our lives to Him. If we're going to see God's dream, the story that He has waiting for us, the only way that can happen is when we let Him write. The story He'll write will be unique for each of us because "no one else can be who you are meant to be. You *are* the hero in your story."[10] It's His story that's written just for Him and you, and He calls you to surrender the pen and participate with Him in the adventure.

Okay, so consider this perspective for a moment. Each of us can think of someone in our circle of influence that is stuck in the sacrifice mode and if that person's a believer when he dies, he will meet God and my guess is that that person's perspective will change. He will see things differently. Can you imagine the look on his face when God sits down with him and reveals the story He wanted to write for his life and he sees how much bigger and more exciting and meaningful it would have been than the life he lived affected by sacrificial stuckitis.[11] He'd be so disappointed at what he missed out on. Talk about a missed opportunity.

Then, imagine those who were daring enough to push themselves into living a life of obedience, more than likely a lot fewer in numbers than those stuck in sacrifice mode. These stories would be much larger and more interesting to read about than the previous group. I wonder how God would read the stories of their lives. There would probably be a few

---

[10] Eldredge, *Wild at Heart,* 142.

[11] John 10:25 "Jesus answered them, I have told you so, yet you do not believe Me [you do not trust Me and rely on Me]. The very works that I do by the power of My Father and in My Father's name bear witness concerning Me [they are My credentials and evidence in support of Me]." (AMP).

more chapters in it about the times when He partnered with them to do things that were really something. But then they'd get to the chapters of the story of their life, the ones that never happened because they never fully let go of the pen, they never surrendered it all and let God write it for them. Then God fills in those blank pages with what He wanted to write for their lives. When He reads them the completed story, the one He wanted to write about their lives, they're blown away by what they could have had.

Then, imagine the few who at some point in their lives fully surrendered the pen to God and said, "Write your story for me, Lord. Wherever, whatever, however, I give it to you." This group of people is smaller than the other groups and God's voice grows louder with excitement as He reads their story to all those gathered. There are no blank pages, no chapters left unread, unparticipated in, or that did not come to fruition. Each chapter had become reality, and everyone is completely amazed at the story. Rick Warren says that surrendering to God "is not passive resignation, fatalism, or an excuse for laziness. It is not accepting the status quo. It may mean the exact opposite: sacrificing your life or suffering in order to change what needs to be changed. God often calls surrendered people to do battle on his behalf. Surrendering is not for cowards or doormats."[12] Handing the pen over to God may in fact be one of, if not *the*, hardest and most dangerous thing you'll ever do.

In the movie *Walk the Line* (the story about Johnny

---

[12] Warren, *The Purpose Driven Life,* 80.

Cash),[13] there's a scene where Johnny Cash has finally stepped out to follow his dream of recording his first record. He's been looking for his opportunity to do just that and finds himself auditioning before the owner/producer of a record label. He's singing a Jack Davis gospel song that speaks about how Jesus gives his followers a peace within, how it's real, and how they're going to shout it. In the middle of the song the owner interrupts the band instructing them to stop playing. He thanks the band for their time, but the way they sang the song just wouldn't cut it. He says that what they're singing about isn't believable and the world doesn't need another rendition of this song sung the same way that hundreds of others have before. He tells them that what people are looking for are songs that are believable and sung from experiences. The point is driven home when he tells Johnny that if you'd been hit by a truck and were lying in the gutter and if you had one chance to sing one song, a song that people would remember him for before he's dirt, a song that would let God know about his time here on earth, one song that would sum him up, would he really choose that song and sing it that way? That's a great question for all of us to ask ourselves.

What's the one unique song that we would sing before God that would sum up our life here on earth? It begs the question. Would the song be the same song that others have sung that's not believable and based on someone else's experiences? Or, would you rather write a brand new song, one from your heart and uniquely written by the ink of experiences that you and God have shared together? Your

---

[13] Twentieth Century Fox Film Corporation, Fox 2000 Pictures, 2005.

song and mine can only be written once we've handed the pen over to God and let Him write His adventure and dream for our lives. Songs are written from experiences, and life is just a word until you live it.[14] From letting God write His dream for us and participating in that dream we are able to write and then sing the one song that we could play before God that would bring praise to the only one worthy ... Him.

Part of the story that God waits to write for each of us could in fact have a musical element to it. After all, He created music as a universal language, and there are almost one hundred references to music and/or instruments in the Bible. Music is one of the ways through which God gets our attention.

When we were discerning whether God was calling us to move to Windsor, both Deb and I noticed one specific song that kept playing. We'd get in the car and turn the radio on and that song would be playing. Switch the station and the same song would be playing. When we were signing the lease to rent the Pastor's Palace, that same song was playing over the sound system in the house at the very moment we were signing our names to the lease. When we pulled out of the driveway of our house for the last time as we headed off to Windsor, the song was playing on the radios in both our cars, even though they were tuned into different stations. The song was about how our lives are made up of the little moments of time and little steps of faith and it became obvious to us that God was all over this decision to step out in faith and move to Windsor. It was part of His story that He was writing in our lives.

[14]   Jason McCoy, "I've Got The Scars To Prove It", Open Road Records, 2008.

Similarly, in early 2008, during the time of discerning what God was trying to tell us, one song seemed to be playing all the time, and its theme was about going home. If God were to write a song for you, right now, something that would get your attention and stir you to hear what He's calling you to do, what would its theme be? Could there perhaps be something that He's doing musically, right now, to get your attention and you haven't really listened for it. Maybe it's time to seek Him.

The larger question for each of us to wrestle with asking ourselves is, what's our one song? What song would we sing that would not only sum up our lives, but would speak of the things we had given up to seek the one thing in our lives that has the greatest meaning and significance, God.[15] The band Finger 11 has a song called, "One Thing," and it asks the question, "What would be the one thing that we would give everything away for?" That's a great question. So, what would it be? Would it be for financial security, toys, houses, prestige, success or anything in between or would it be for one chance to experience God writing His dream for our lives? The answer to that one question is found when we move from obedience to surrender.

Deb and I continued to do all the checklist items in discerning what God was doing or calling us to do. We sought

---

[15] Psalm 105:1 "Hallelujah! Thank God! Pray to him by name! Tell everyone you meet what he has done! Sing him songs, belt out hymns, translate his wonders into music! Honor his holy name with Hallelujahs, you who seek God. Live a happy life! Keep your eyes open for God, watch for his works; be alert for signs of his presence. Remember the world of wonders he has made, his miracles, and the verdicts he's rendered—O seed of Abraham, his servant, O child of Jacob, his chosen." *The Message.*

Him through His Word, constant prayer, journaling, discussing it with our spiritual mentors, other believers, non-believers, as well as our kids who were fine with either option—although our daughter leaned toward coming back—but there was unity in the family at wherever God wanted us to be. We continued the conversation with my boss and his wife. We shared with them our growing sense that God was calling us back home and while they still didn't see all the elements and they were not fully on board with God's call since it didn't make sense to them, they were walking with us through the discernment process. We totally understood their position because on the one hand it didn't make any sense that we would be called down to Windsor for such a short time, but on the other hand He could be doing a new thing in His congregation, something that might not have been thought of or visible at the time, but something that God wanted them as a group to go through together by way of my leaving.

Consider Paul's ministry for a minute. He stayed in Antioch with Barnabas for one year. His first missionary journey lasted nine months and he visited many different cities over that span. He was in Corinth for a little over a year, Ephesus for around two years. God called Paul, and the other disciples, to many different spots and they just went never asking the question of, "How long will I be there, Lord" or, "What's been done in the past?" They just handed over the pen and followed God's lead.

Our conversations about us leaving would have been easier to have if there was any type of conflict going on between pastor and associate. There wasn't. It could have been easier if I was being directly called to another church, but I wasn't so it made the foundation of understanding and acceptance that God was in fact doing something difficult at times for them to embrace. We continued to wait on God for direction, we'd handed Him the pen and surrendered everything to Him. Our prayer was to just take the distractions away and make it clear and to start writing the next chapter of His story, His dream for us.

I have spoken about the times when God steps out first and makes things really clear as to what will happen to make it very obvious that He's calling His people in a certain direction. Then there are times when He tells us to step out in faith, first, and then He will deliver on His promises by revealing what's next. I've also spoken about how growing in our connection with God means that we move from putting down fleeces to hearing God's call to step out in faith and how He wants us to get in sync with his heartbeat and hear His call to do just that.

Well, in a quiet morning of prayer, I heard the call, "Go forward." Nothing more. But I knew it was Him and He'd spoken. However, the instruction "Go forward" was vague. Go forward where? It's been my experience that God uses simple words and phrases to spark a curiosity to find Him and clarification in His word. In its Hebrew root "Go forward" is used to describe human motion in the process of life's journey by moving and not staying still. It's a way of calling us into and testing our faithfulness to God.[16] It's one

---

[16] William D. Mounce, *Mounce's Complete Expository Dictionary of Old and New Testament Words,* (Grand Rapids, MI: Zondervan, 2006), 290–291.

of the ways God reveals His presence and calls us to travel with Him as He answers our cry for Him to show us His ways, to teach us His paths, to show us how to live.[17] It's about getting in sync with His heartbeat. To walk with God on His pathway for our lives, means that we are constantly surrendered and dependent on Him "for each step along the path of righteousness requires his direction ... our dependence on God for it is a journey traveled together with him."[18]

Within a week of hearing the call to "Go Forward" I hear, again, the instruction to "Go forward ... Go forward into the unknown ... faith is going forward into the unknown ... like Abraham ... it's time to go!" Moments like these are cemented in my memories. They're times when you actually hear the voice and prompting by the almighty God (El Shaddai) and while there's no pressure to respond, there's just the invitation to answer the call. The call to dig deeper into His Word, the call to surrender and trust, the call to do something in total faith even though I don't know exactly what it is, yet. It's the call to surrender the pen. So, I went into His Word and read about Abraham.

Abraham lived at a time when most people ignored God. They were happily doing their thing and Abraham's life was just fine the way it was. It's not like he was unhappy or suffering or he didn't have shelter or food or whatever. He was immersed in the routine of comfort. Do you think people within the community doubted Abraham's actions when he

---

[17] Psalm 25:4 "Show me the right path, O LORD; point out the road for me to follow." (NLT) and Psalm 25:4 "Show me how you work, GOD; School me in your ways." *The Message.*

[18] Mounce, Mounce's Complete Expository, 291.

explained that God had told him to pick everything up and go without knowing where he was going to go? You bet they did. Some would have cheered him on, others would have scoffed at his claim that God spoke. His openness to following God's call didn't matter to anyone else but Abraham as he heard God tell him to do something that made no sense. But he could not shake the fact that he had heard! God just told him to "go" and he had no idea where he and his family were going or what he was going to do, or what they would wear, or eat ... nothing. He just knew that he had heard God's call and he had to follow it.

Later on, God called Abraham to give back and sacrifice his only son, Isaac. The command didn't make sense, but Abraham responded out of surrendered faith. God stops him just before he does it, but the reality is that God was testing his faith.[19] God tests us[20] and if hearing Him call me to go forward was a test from God, I knew that I wanted to pass. Tests of faith have a way of further defining, forming, and purifying our character[21] and, as I headed out to work that morning, the words "you'll know when you know" played in my mind and I knew that I had to tell my boss that I'd heard and I had to go.

Testing of our faith happens at different phases of life's

---

[19] Genesis 22:1–2 "Some time later God tested Abraham. He said to him, "Abraham!" "Here I am," he replied. 2 Then God said, "Take your son, your only son, Isaac, whom you love, and go to the region of Moriah. Sacrifice him there as a burnt offering on one of the mountains I will tell you about." (NIV).

[20] 1 Thessalonians 2:3 "God tested us thoroughly to make sure we were qualified to be trusted with this Message. Be assured that when we speak to you we're not after crowd approval—only God approval." *The Message*.

[21] Psalm 66:10 "For you, O God, tested us; you refined us like silver." (NIV).

journey. The sacrifice level—what we do or don't do—is based on fear masked as reluctance to really step out and live the way God calls us to live. We justify this reluctance by keeping a ledger of everything we've given up or that we've done or accomplished for God. It's here that God tests our heart's desire to stop keeping score.

The obedience level is where God has made it completely obvious as to where He wants us to go and what to do and all we have to do is to respond to the call. He tests our faith here, too, as these little steps build our character and confidence, all the while opening the channel for us to feel and experience a small portion of God's heartbeat for us.

The deepest level—surrender—is where God wants each of us to walk with Him continually. This is where we give Him the pen to write His story for us and these moments of faith are the key building blocks for growing a heart that beats after God's. When we truly understand that by giving God the pen, the one we hold so tightly in our hands, the one pen that's assigned and uniquely made just for each of us, the only pen that holds the ink used for writing the story of our lives, we see things differently and our visual and spiritual peripheral vision is expanded. We know if left alone and in total control of writing our stories we'd end up writing something that was well thought out, structural, straight, comfortable, and for the most part very safe. If, however, we could rewrite our story after getting just a small glimpse into how God would write it, there's no doubt that we'd go back and change how our original story read. It would be more exciting, faster paced, and way more interesting to tell others about, right? That's the way God writes. It's biblical. He's God and He calls us to surrender the pen and let Him write our stories.

Surrendering the pen also means giving him our desire to maintain control of writing the story and so we step into the vulnerability of being written into a much larger story. It's in the weakness of vulnerability that God does great and amazing things through us and we become stronger than before. It means that we step out in faith: sure of what we hope for (God to move through us) and certain of what we do not see (the active participation of God's Kingdom here on earth, the writing of the story) in powerful ways that change our lives, but also change the lives of those around us and in the next generation. God's great stories, written through our desire to answer His call, become part of the collection of stories that are told generation after generation.[22] Those people who have surrendered their lives by going forward in faith have been mightily used by God to do the humanly unthinkable and impossible. They answered the call with great excitement by responding with "You want me to ... *what?*"[23]

When it was announced to staff that I would be leaving, it was obvious the effect that that news had on a team. God had put together a phenomenal team at this church and they, along with the congregation, had gone through a lot of

---

[22] Hebrews 11:2 "Faith is the reason we remember great people who lived in the past." (NCV).

[23] Hebrews 11:33–34 "By faith these people overthrew kingdoms, ruled with justice, and received what God had promised them. They shut the mouths of lions, 34 quenched the flames of fire, and escaped death by the edge of the sword. Their weakness was turned to strength. They became strong in battle and put whole armies to flight." (NLT)

changes since the transition of leadership and things were really starting to gel. You could see it in the team, elders, and the congregation. The staff and leadership of Lakeshore were just starting to catch momentum and everyone was looking forward to the next phase or chapter in the story of God's church at this location. But God had other things planned. We announced my departure to both the staff and elders on the same day, and it was hard. The plan was to announce it to the congregation on the coming Sunday. I was not looking forward to the congregation having to go through more change and I knew some would find it hard because they had, in a very short period of time, secured a special spot in my family's heart.

Every Friday afternoon during my time at Lakeshore, I walked into the auditorium just to spend some time with God in prayer. This became a bit of special time for me to hear from Him and it was on the Friday before we were to announce my departure to the congregation that God gave me a phenomenal vision. I was praying for the congregation and for the right words to be said on the coming Sunday and for those words to be heard the right way and throughout my time in prayer the enemy was doing his best to fire arrows of doubt my way. I was calling out for God to take this element away and to confirm that I was not off base, as some would think, but that His call was for me to respond like Abraham and go. After making that request things got quiet all around me. Then God started to paint an amazing picture.

Along both sides of the center aisle of the auditorium, angels appeared, glowingly white as freshly fallen snow, and they formed a path from the stage area where I was praying and rose up and floated in the air high above. They all played trumpets and formed a path that led down both sides of the center aisle and out the two main doors of the auditorium where they turned left and continued out of the main doorway of the church. It was an answer to prayer and I thanked God so much for that vision because I knew that I'd heard Him call me and that would be the beginning of many signs of affirmation that our stepping out in faith was surrendering to God's call. We had handed over the pen not knowing where or what the next chapter would look like, but knowing that we were headed back to the Barrie area.

Sunday arrived and when it came time to announce my plans to leave it caught many by surprise. This congregation had already gone through many different layers of change and now just when things were settling in I was going to cause some more change. I knew this would be met with some different reactions. Living a life surrendered to God means that things will not always make sense or that your decision(s) to follow God's call could be met with different reactions by those affected by your decision. Answering God's call means that you'll be changed as a result of the experience of stepping out and pursuing God's call—and so will others. Whether you're going to answer God's call to come into a relationship with His son, or to move from sacrifice to obedience to complete surrender, the experience itself will change you and will also impact those around you because they'll be forced to deal with the boundary changes of your decision.

When we are faced with the concerns that change exposes

us to, we must observe our own reactions and ask why we're feeling and reacting the way we are about the change. If we ask God to reveal what He wants to teach us in that moment, the revelation that we receive will heighten our awareness and discernment of the nuances that God is incorporating into His story for our lives. "The church is God's agent of change through which his power is revealed ... and we are not only called to be changed and to embrace change but to be the catalysts of that change."[24]

One of my favorite television ads is entitled, "Think Different," and it was created by Macintosh computers. It shows several people in our history who have dared to dream and think outside the box and, despite the obstacles they would face along the road to pursuing that dream, they challenged us to think differently. The ad says these people were motivated by something deep inside of them, a dream, and whether you liked them or not they were people who moved beyond the status quo. They were rebels and misfits, and regardless how you felt about them you just couldn't ignore them because they changed things. They pushed the human race forward.

Isn't that what Jesus did with his disciples? Isn't that what the early church did? They changed the boundaries of culture's comfort zone. They stepped outside the boundaries of the status quo. They changed things by pushing the human race towards Jesus. "The first-century church didn't keep up with its time, didn't spend its energy keeping up with its time. The first-century church changed time. But it

---

[24] McManus, *An Unstoppable Force,* 89.

rewrote history. It radically impacted culture. The church was the forerunner, not the runner-up."[25] The church is the test tube where God unleashes change so that we, the church, will have firsthand experience with change and will expand that change to the community around us. Whenever things change around us we need to rearrange the boundaries of our own comfort zone. If we answer God's call to draw closer to Him then things around us will change and there will be a variety of reactions, but all of us will learn from the stepping out as "daring faith is contagious."[26]

Wilkinson outlines four types of people in Ordinary's life who will negatively react to his prompting to pursue his dream. The alarmist thinks everything new is dangerous and unsafe. The traditionalist romanticizes the past and is motivated to keep things the way they are by custom and routine. The defeatist thinks nothing is possible and sees problems everywhere. And the antagonist, whose motivation to resist change is based on jealousy and loss of control.

When you decide to answer God's call and pursue His dream for you, you might meet some of these people in your own circle of influence. Don't despair. Rather, understand where their discomfort comes from. It's not personal, it's just that your actions have altered the boundaries of their comfort zone and that makes them uncomfortable. They have to deal with change that has been initiated from outside of their comfort zone. "For many people even deep dissatisfaction with the known present can be preferable to the fear of the

---

[25] Ibid, 66.

[26] Ortberg, *If You Want to Walk on Water,* 133.

unknown future. I learned that when people are afraid, they turn inward to protect themselves and those things most personal and important to them."[27]

In Proverbs 29:25[28] it's written that "the fear of human opinion disables; trusting in God protects you from that." Our human nature resists change, and perhaps the only person who wholeheartedly looks forward to and embraces change is a baby with a wet diaper. If we're going to pursue God's call on our lives there will be tests along the journey of discovering exactly what that call looks like, and these tests are what the disciple Paul wrote about when he said, "God tested us thoroughly to make sure we were qualified to be trusted with this Message. Be assured that when we speak to you we're not after crowd approval—only God approval."[29]

Once the decision had been announced and we had "let go," trusting God, things started to move very quickly. During this time of transition, and packing for a third move in fourteen months, God gave us little cheers or holy high-fives along the way to keep us focused on His activity instead of negativity or doubt. He gave Deb and I more visions about what the future might hold, but never clearly showing us the specifics of what lay ahead. This taught us to trust in Him even though we could not see what the next step looked like. In moments of transition like this, we had to be aware that our "preoccupation with what lies ahead betrays a desire to

---

[27] Carly Fiorina, *Tough Choices—A Memoir,* (New York, NY: Penguin Group, 2006), 121.

[28] *The Message.*

[29] 1 Thessalonians 2:3 *The Message.*

control a future that simply cannot be controlled. We want the security of knowing what the future will bring rather than risk trusting God as the unknown future gradually unfolds itself before us. We keep hoping that light will shine to illuminate the entire journey ahead so that we will know everything there is to know about the future, and thus be spared the difficulty of having to trust God. Ironically, we want to know so much about the future that we won't even have to trust God anymore."[30]

God was teaching us a whole different level of trusting in Him and one of the key texts for us during this entire period was from Proverbs: "Trust God from the bottom of your heart; don't try to figure out everything on your own. Listen for God's voice in everything you do, everywhere you go; he's the one who will keep you on track."[31] So, that's exactly what we did.

Meanwhile, we had put the "for sale" sign on the front lawn of our new house and God was bringing a lot of prospective purchasers through in a market that was getting softer by the day. We had to trust that God would bring a buyer soon and we were also trusting in Him to provide a spot for us to rent back home since we had not sold our house in Windsor. He ended up providing a beautiful place for us to rent back in the same school area as before when absolutely nothing was on the market to rent.

Deb approached every house that was listed for sale in our old area inquiring if the owners would be interested in renting

---

[30] Sittser, *The Will of God,* 27.

[31] Proverbs 3:5–6 *The Message.*

their homes. Every one of the agents came back with solid "no's." We grew a little concerned as our moving date was fast approaching when Deb got an email from one of the agents she contacted who had a friend who had a friend ... and this owner was looking at traveling for a year and even though his house was not on the market, nor did anyone know what his plans were, there was the potential that he could be interested in renting, but he'd have to meet us first. We talked about it and agreed that to create the most favorable impression to the owner, we should send the people most equipped to do that— Deb and the kids. The dog and I stayed home.

So, they drove up and met the owner and he really liked them and agreed to rent his house to us. This was a real gift. It was a lot smaller than our previous houses and not as fancy, which was a lesson for both of us and a reminder that our daily bread is all we needed. What this house lacked in material finishing more than made up in opening my eyes to God's creation as it has an amazing view that inspired me each day while writing. This was just one of many little nudges by God that let us know He was cheering us on.

Deb had also been struggling with some health issues that seemed to be getting worse and once we returned to the Barrie area we found out that her doctor was, in fact, one of the leading specialists for her symptoms.

We left Windsor at the end of August, our house still hadn't sold, but we did the Abraham shuffle, stepped out in faith, and went forward trusting and praying for God to do a miracle and sell our house quickly, and lifted this up to God and focused on Him. It was tough to step out, again, as all the economic signs indicated that a major correction was looming on the horizon not to mention that our house was located in the worst selling market in Canada. Nonetheless we continued to trust in Him and we stepped out and moved back. We had to continue to put our faith into action and this step was a strong reminder for us that "faith that counts, then, is not the absence of doubt; it's the presence of action. It puts you into motion, propels you to action."[32] We shuffled back to Barrie. Within five weeks of stepping out in faith, moving back and leaving it up to God to affirm, He did. An offer came in for our house that closed within two weeks of acceptance and it all happened in a market where the average selling time, if a house sells at all, was almost 500 days. God answers those who step out in faith and then wait for Him to act.[33]

One of the most poignant moments for me was immediately after preaching my last service at Lakeshore. I'd had the opportunity to share with the congregation some of the details surrounding our decision to step out in faith and I tried to the best of my ability to share some of the thresholds we encountered as we came to the decision to, once again, step out and follow His call. After I had finished, the congregation responded loudly and I knew that the majority had given us their blessing. It confirmed for me that all of God's people are open to and longing for the opportunity to cheer on, love, and support movements done where we

---

[32] Brian D. McLaren, *The Secret Message of Jesus—Uncovering the Truth That Could Change Everything,* (Nashville, TN: W Publishing Group, 2006), 109.

[33] Psalm 37:7 "Be still in the presence of the LORD, and wait patiently for him to act." (NLT).

surrender ourselves to God's call and respond by putting our faith into action. "Faith is something to be experienced and exercised, not defined, categorized, and neatly packaged"[34] and we long for moments to encourage and participate in situations where God is moving and doing a brand new thing.

On this Sunday, however, God spoke very clearly to me and it was in a quiet but oh-so-powerful moment. One of the long-standing members of Lakeshore St. Andrew's, a real matriarch and stake holder, gently touched my hand and asked for a moment with me. I gladly accepted the invitation and as she pulled me closer so that I could hear, she said that she knew Lakeshore wouldn't keep me here for long and while she'd truly enjoyed my teaching—then with a sparkle in her eyes she got real close to me and continued, "but perhaps the greatest teaching you've given us is showing us firsthand our need to always be open to stepping out in faith and actually doing it." Here was a lady who, for so many years had participated in many different steps of faith with this congregation, and yet she was inspired by the story that God was writing through me and my family. Praise God!

Handing the pen over to God and letting Him write what He wants to write through all of us shifts our hearts and eyes to become more closely aligned with His. Remember the words of Mark Twain: "Twenty years from now you will be more disappointed by the things that you didn't do than by the ones you did do. So throw off the bowlines. Sail away from the safe harbor. Catch the trade winds in your sails.

---

[34] Sheila Walsh, *Extraordinary Faith,* (Nashville, TN: Nelson Books, 2005), 53.

Explore. Dream. Discover."

God rewards and blesses surrender. Deb, the kids, and I were returning home from a trip out West when we experienced the blessings of surrendering and trusting in God to work things out. We were returning from a skiing trip in the Rockies and our flight home left the Calgary airport at 6:30 a.m. so that we could get home nice and early to get everything coordinated before everyone got back into their routines. It was the day before everyone was scheduled to return to school and work from the Christmas vacation so the airport was a complete and utter chaos. There were people everywhere even at 4:30 a.m. What we found was beyond busy. We got to the check-in counter for our flight after an hour in line to be told that our flight had been cancelled and we were going to be bumped to the next available flight which was at 3:45 that afternoon. That didn't sit well with us not to mention the hundreds of other travelers who felt the same way, and as each person was told the same thing tension mounted and eventually exploded as the people behind us realized what was happening. It was at this moment that we began to pray while trying our best not to get sucked into the emotions of others by remaining calm even though both of us knew that we had to get back that day.

We didn't have the luxury of getting bumped and then possibly getting bumped again. This was definitely a test, and testing "comes into our lives to make us more flexible, to stretch us out of our comfort zone. God stretches us by taking us into the territory we do not naturally feel comfortable in. When we move in a direction that is not our natural reaction

... it brings about maturity. We do not grow by staying in our comfort zone."[35]

God was sure testing our patience and comfort zone and anything else because at that time of the morning after little sleep the night before I was out of my comfort zone and starting to panic like everyone else. My old ways told me to raise my voice and make a scene like someone important, but a calmness came over both of us and as we silently lifted up this situation in prayer. We were very calm and polite to the person working behind the counter. She very patiently explained the dilemma and I patiently listened and then I patiently explained my side of the story. She smiled at me and patiently listened. After listening to my side of the story she then started to explain her side of the story, again, which I listened to very patiently, again, while continuing to pray. My patient exterior and kind understanding words were clearly not working as she tagged our tickets with these bright orange special stickers that signified that we had lost our seats and were now being bumped to the possibility of another flight, but with no guarantees that we would get on a flight home that day.

We patiently listened to and then followed her instructions and went over to the special counter that she directed us to and got another different colored sticker placed on our tickets and then we were directed into the waiting area where all the other people who had been bumped were now congregating. The tension began to grow very quickly. The waiting area

---

[35] Mike Breen and Walt Kallestad, *The Passionate Church, The Art of Life Changing Discipleship,* (Colorado Springs, CO: NexGen, 2005), 153.

began to look like that of exiles from different lands all gathering in one spot and all wanting to tell anyone who would listen how they should not be trapped in this situation. Each new person from the other bumped flights proceeded to the ticket counter and explained who they were and why they needed to get on that flight and how important they were and how their name was so and so and they wanted to speak to the person in charge as to why they had been so humiliated at having been bumped when they flew this airline all the time and do you know who I am ...

The stories were non-stop and all of them had the same components. Everyone wanted to use their own efforts to get something done and I must admit that I wanted to do the very same thing and show everyone else in that stifling and over crowded waiting area that I, too, was someone and just watch my efforts in getting this done ... my way ... by my efforts ... to impress everyone else with my abilities and preferred status.

By now our patience was really being tested and we were starting to wonder if God was even hearing our prayers. Tension was building and then one of the kids waiting in the area, whose parents were busy telling anyone who would listen just how really important they were, decided to open their violin case and take out their violin and play their rendition of some Mozart song that sounded exactly like the song called "finger nails being dragged down the chalk board." It was not only unbearable, but it was becoming painful to sit still as we really wanted to join in the lobbying. We looked at each other and decided to surrender the whole thing up to God to let Him work it all out. We both just gave it up to God and waited. This was really hard for me as I trusted more in my abilities than God's desire to work things out His way.

Just before the plane was to leave the terminal, there was a mad rush and last minute lobbying scramble to get on that plane, but as we just sat there waiting for God to direct and work things out we remained surrendered to His will in this moment. We were totally surrendered to Him moving, in His way and time. At the last minute, they called our names out and we stood and walked through the scowl of many people who were indignantly upset that they weren't called and as we handed our tickets to the person behind the counter another different colored tag was placed on our tickets and as the person behind the counter handed the tickets to my daughter he said, "Now you make sure you enjoy your seats." We proceeded down the ramp to the plane where we were seated in four seats, all of them first class, to make it back home in time. You should have seen the look on our kids faces!

You should have seen the look on all of our faces as I learned that my efforts can accomplish nothing when it's all about me. However, when we surrender ourselves to God's plan for each moment of our lives He does hear our prayers and answers them in ways that we would never have dreamed of or anticipated. God blesses those who surrender the direction of their lives to His way, timing, direction, outcome, and you "know you're surrendered to God when you rely on God to work things out instead of trying to manipulate others, force your agenda, and control the situation. You let go and let God work."[36]

Growing deeper in our relationship with God happens when our action of obedience, handing Him the pen, intersects with our attitude of great anticipation at what lies ahead. Surrender the pen this very moment. You know the one you've been using to write the story of your life? Surrender it to God, hand it over to Him and let Him start writing His dream for you. You can never anticipate or expect the blessing, journey or the path that God wants to give those who surrender all of their lives to seeking Him and following His leading. Your life will never be the same and you'll be blessed beyond belief by doing it.

---

[36] Warren, *The Purpose Driven Life,* 80–81.

Chapter 11

I WILL

"Our lives are really about events connected together over time and our response to these events."[1]

"Our deep sense of calling should send us on a journey of discovery. We have to travel to get to where God wants us to go. It is not an easy path we must follow." Jerry Sittser

Do you remember those moments in your life when you witnessed history in the making? Each of us has different moments in our life that are etched in our memories and, while they're significant to us, they may or may not have the same significance to others.

Then there are those moments when everyone in our lives and those in the greater circle of our relationships witness something that the collective community shares together, and such stories are retold year after year and they weave a common thread through the hearts and souls of everyone there. These could be the family stories that are retold every Christmas; and while the stories get embellished each year, so, too, does the sound of the laughter that erupts at the retelling. The moment the story unfolded before us never fades from our memories. These moments bring people together, if but

---

[1] Breen and Kallestad, *The Passionate Church,* 53.

for a brief time. These can also be painful moments where we bury the hurt and try to avoid any mention of the moment itself ever having happened.

Then, there are the moments when a larger community or even a country gathers together to experience and witness something special happening. If you're a Canadian, then one of your moments could be "the goal" that Paul Henderson scored for Team Canada to beat the Russians. I can remember our teacher bringing a television into our classroom so we could all watch the game and experience history in the making. If you're an American, then perhaps one of the moments could be the miracle on ice when Team USA beat the Russians to win the Olympic gold medal in men's hockey.

Then there are the moments when the world watches together and we as a global people celebrate our accomplishments, but also experience together a moment that is written in our history. Perhaps one such moment is watching the first step that man made on the moon. What is most intriguing for me is the acknowledgement of the potential that awaits just before the historical moment happens. It's the moment just before history is written that we're invited to participate in as it unfolds. These are *right here ... right now* moments. When a gathering of people have collectively shifted their focus to one thing with each life sitting on the edge of their seat with great excitement and anticipation of what is to take place and the hope the event inspires everyone to have.

Recently, all of us were invited into such a moment: November 4, 2008. Location: Grant Park in Chicago, Illinois.

Thousands gathered in the park to experience history in the making and millions gathered by television or Internet to join in the historical moment. Barack Obama would address the people gathered in the park and those watching as he secured his place in history as the first African American to be elected President of the United States. Regardless of one's political or religious agendas, the majority of the world stopped whatever it was they were doing and gathered in great anticipation and excitement at the invitation into the story of history being written. We don't forget moments like those because we're allowed to participate in the event while the event itself changes our lives and that of others as it brings us hope. Hope that things will change for the better. Hope that there is, in fact, something else out there that will fill the void in our lives. Hope that there is healing in a world that is hurting so much. Hope that there is a power far greater than the evil we see all around us. The victory of hope.

These types of moments happened throughout the Bible, as well. Any time Jesus and his disciples gathered, there was the expectation that something significant was going to happen. People would be healed and hope would be given to everyone watching as the living God created powerful and wonderful experiences that touched and changed people's lives. People gathered because they knew that history was unfolding right before them and they wanted to participate in the hope, power, and love that God-ordained significant moments in time have on our souls. They would retell these stories to future generations so they, too, would hear about Jesus and be invited to experience the story He wants to write in and through all of us. These types of moments are defined in the Bible as kairos moments and they're right here ... right now moments.

Even today, we long for kairos moments because they change us by filling the holes in our lives with potential, possibility and hope that we can experience something that will affect us, and reorient our compass bearing to true north toward meaning, purpose, acceptance, and love. It's found at the experience of the cross. Can you imagine what it would look like if people gathered on a regular basis in anticipation of experiencing an event where they would see and participate in lives changed forever? It would be awesome.

The beginning of this book had a story about a person hanging on for dear life and desperately calling out for someone to help them. God answers their cry, but instructs them to do something that is dangerous and risky. He calls them to let go of everything and to trust in Him and Him alone to rescue them. The ending of the story is not completed because it's waiting for each of us to participate in the story. The story is our story and wherever you are right now in your life, there is a still small voice that is calling you to let go and trust Him. As we broaden the perspective of the story and pull back a little further it reveals a larger group of people who join the story and watch how and what you do with God's command to "Let Go!" There's a crowd gathering to watch how things unfold and while they're all focused on you for this brief moment, they, too, are going through the very same thing in some part of their lives. They're struggling with whether or not to follow Jesus and waiting to see how trustworthy God will be. They're waiting and watching how you react to God's call because it will have great influence on them.

There could be others watching you, right now, who are stuck in their own sacrificial stuckitis that has been holding them back for so long from truly following the path that God is calling them to journey along with Him. They may be just on the edge of finally letting go and following after God's heart, but they're afraid to really trust God because they're afraid of being exposed and somehow they've bought into the notion that God, and others, will see just how vulnerable and broken they really are. We're all, in some form or another, broken as a result of living in a sinful world, but at this moment your actions will blaze a path towards regeneration and hope of a better day in their lives. Your actions will be sparks of motivation for them to finally get unstuck from all of the baggage that has been holding them back for so long and finally let Jesus heal them. If you let go and trust God's call, others in the gathering crowd will find the courage to do the very same thing.

There could be those gathering in the crowd who long ago stopped trusting in God and have just been comfortably coasting through this life. They're content to be cheering you on to answer God's call while hoping that God doesn't call them out of the comforts of their routines to do something brand new. Yet perhaps at this very moment your ability to completely surrender the pen of your life's story and hand it over to God will be enough of a catalyst to move someone from the comforts of mere obedience to the adventure of surrender.

God is calling His people and His church to kairos moments that He's orchestrating in each of our lives. He invites us to embrace them with our actions that will inspire a similar response in those who are watching us. "The destinies of many people depend on how you respond to God."[2] This invitation from God is custom made, uniquely designed, for each of us and it sits waiting to be opened and lived out loud! There will always be those who will miss the kairos moments of their lives and they will go to their graves very sad and bitter people who have missed out on the great adventure that God wanted to write in and through them. The imminence of one's death has a way of awakening one's senses to the significance of the lost opportunity of right here ... right now moments. However, by the time that realization has occurred it's too late to do anything about it, the opportunities have been lost and they die willing to do anything to get those moments back, longing for another chance.

If you were in such a moment like that and you were given another chance to do things over again, would you? Would you pursue that dream that God has been stirring in your soul? If you knew that there were people gathering with great excitement, that God was going to reveal His dream for someone and it ended up being given to you, how would you respond to the dream? Would you run up to get the dream from God and then turn around and on your way to your seat you look up and see all of the people waiting for you to take hold of that dream and do something with it?

---

[2]   Sunday Andelaja, *Church Shift,* (Lake Mary, FL: Charisma House, 2008), 100.

Larry Walters was a truck driver who lived near the Los Angeles airport and for twenty years he had a dream about traveling into the clear blue sky in a weather balloon. So on July 2, 1982, he bought forty-five helium-filled weather balloons and decided with the help of some friends that he would tie them to a lawn chair and let the balloons carry him towards his dream. He called his homemade contraption "Inspiration I" and on launch day he gathered his BB gun figuring that if he went too high he could just shoot a couple of balloons and come back down. He called out to his ground crew to let go and very quickly rose at over a thousand feet per minute to an altitude of over sixteen thousand feet. He lost the BB gun and the first person to see Larry was the pilot of a TWA flight coming into LAX international. Can you imagine the look on the pilot's face to see some guy holding on for dear life to a lawn chair tied to a bunch of weather balloons? Can you imagine the look on Larry's face! He shut down air traffic for several hours and, when they finally rescued him he was asked why he did it and he responded, "A man just can't sit there."[3]

That's so true for our lives and the dreams that God has waiting for us. We just can't sit there! Larry knew that if he didn't do something about what was stirring in his heart he'd miss the opportunity, he'd miss the moment and he knew that it was too great a moment to miss out on and to have die inside of him. But because he did something about it, his story is still told, today. He did something and his actions influenced and inspired others to do something, as well.

---

[3] Wendy Northcutt, The Darwin Awards, (New York, NY: Plume/ The Penguin Group, 2002), 281.

The same is true for all of us, particularly as it centers on hearing God's call on our lives and the degree of trust that we hope for in God's desire to participate in our lives. That's what faith is. Hebrews 11:1–3 reads that the "fundamental fact of existence is that this trust in God, this faith, is the firm foundation under everything that makes life worth living. It's our handle on what we can't see. The act of faith is what distinguished our ancestors, set them above the crowd. By faith, we see the world called into existence by God's word, what we see created by what we don't see."[4]

The unseen God speaks and creates the seen. The unseen God calls out to each of us to let go of trying to control our lives and let Him write and create the evidence of our faith in Him. Such evidence is a powerful and inspiring witness to those seeking kairos moments in their lives. These are moments when one's faith no longer sits idle like a thing or object that can be hung up in a closet and taken out every now and again. No. Faith is a verb, active and alive, meant to be lived out and witnessed for everyone to see. Active faith results in participating in the unseen becoming visible. Faith remains static as long as we hold on to the branch, hoping that someone else will save us instead of answering God's call to let go. This is not complete faith. Faith only becomes complete when it becomes an active verb. When we hear God call us to let go of our branch and we do so, with the assurance that He will catch us and rescue us from our dilemma. It's in the rescuing that our faith becomes seen not only by ourselves, but those around us who are watching.

---

[4]   *The Message*

This type of faith changes not only our relationship with God, but it inspires and motivates others to not just sit there, but to do something! Our relationship with God and the depth of our faith is in the shifting of our response to His call. It's the intentional shift from "?" to "*?*." Instead of responding to God's call on your life with, "You want me to ... *what?*" full of angst, fear, and trepidation, respond with a "You want me to ... *what?*" that's filled with great expectation that something amazing is going to happen and you just can't wait to see what God wants to do in and through you. That's active faith and that's where God wants all of us to be living.

Why? If we're to live and experience a full life here on earth we just can't sit there. We just can't sit there because God "is recruiting people to join a revolutionary movement of change."[5] There are already too many people sitting there waiting for something to happen, they've been waiting for the church to do something, but we've missed the boat. Can you imagine if on any given day people gathered at churches throughout the land with such great excitement and anticipation for what God was going to do that day? What kind of witness would the church be if everyone within the church actually sought God's will regardless of the cost? We wouldn't be able to build big enough buildings to house all of the people who would want to attend such an event.

However, nothing ever happens until someone decides to let go and do something. "Nothing ever happens until someone

---

[5] McLaren, *The Secret Message of Jesus,* 143.

says 'I will.'"[6] That has been the case since the beginning of time when God said, "I will create something out of nothing," and He did. Stories that inspire us to dream and think big only become life changing and timeless when someone says, "I will." The life that each of us has been given is a gift, given to us by a creator—God—who decided that He would create us so that we could choose to be in a relationship with Him. He decided that He would take the first step by doing something and creating our own story for each of us to experience with Him. If we follow His word and "Think Big"[7] we leave room within the story for God to join us and that's way more exciting than if we just sat there and did nothing. Without active faith we miss out on the fullness that He has waiting for us and it then becomes impossible to please Him.[8] Our best efforts combined with His guidance and a response to His call with "I will" becomes a recipe for life transformation in and through us, not to mention that things change as a result of us putting our faith into action. There is a ripple effect on those who are watching us live out our faith.

"The enemy in our time is not human capacity, or over activism, but the enemy is passivity—the idea that God has done everything and you are essentially left to be a consumer of the grace of God ... We all know that Jesus said (in John 15), 'without me you can do nothing.' We need to add, 'if

---

[6] Fred Smith, Sr., *Breakfast With Fred,* (Ventura, CA: Regal Books, 2007), 72.

[7] Isaiah 54:2 *The Message.*

[8] Hebrews 11:6 "Without faith it is impossible to please God, because anyone who comes to him must believe that he exists and that he rewards those who earnestly seek him." (NIV).

you do nothing, it will be most assuredly without him.'"[9] There's too much at stake for us to just sit there and stay comfortable. My hope is that in some small way this book will have been the conduit for those who are feeling and hearing God's call to follow it and do something. Perhaps someone has handed you this book and you have a sense that Jesus Christ is now calling you to step towards him as your Lord and Savior. If that's the case then it's time for you to respond with, "I will give you my life, this day, Jesus, and ask that you come into my heart and lead me toward your call on my life. Please forgive me of my past and start a new life in me, this day and forever more, and I will follow you and seek you with everything I have from this day forward and in Jesus' name ... I will."

This may be the time for you to ask God to clean the ledger you've been using over the past years and to truly fill your heart with the courage and strength to answer His call to let go and fully trust in Him by praying, "This day, Father, I ask that you take the past away from me, erase the ledger of sacrifice that I've been keeping score on and make me aware of the areas in my life that you want to regenerate in me. I will follow your guidance and walk with you wherever you take me. Help me to give you the rest of my heart from this day forward and in Jesus' name I pray ... I will."

This may be the moment when you realize you've been holding on to the pen that's writing your story and you've

---

[9] Dallas Willard Interviewed by Andy Peck for *Christianity + Renewal Magazine* http://www.dwillard.org/articles/artview.asp?artid=92, UK, May 2002. Accessed May 11, 2009.

been doing it for too long and you can no longer ignore the stirring within you. It's a discontent and you're struck by the open acknowledgement that you have been playing it safe and comfortable for too long. Perhaps now is the time for you to say, "Father, I ask you to give me the strength to surrender to you, this day, the pen that I've been controlling and writing the story of my life with. I hereby surrender it totally and completely to you and ask that you write your story in my life. Forgive me for drifting away from you and I ask that you give me the strength and courage to change my direction and draw me back to you, keep me focused and guided on seeking your path and direction for me, this day and forever more. I will actively seek your call to let go and completely surrender my agenda to your will for my life. I ask this in Jesus' precious name ... and I hereby commit to answering your call on my life with ... I will."

Lord, our common prayer this day is to ask that you write a new thing in our lives, something that will bring you praise and glory so that others will follow our lead and they, too, will be powerfully affected and drawn into a deeper relationship with you. Lord, may we all see your signs, wonders and miracles, again, so that our children and future generations will see your glory at work in and through us. May we continue to understand and experience your awesome love for all of us. Grant us the privilege to participate with you, here, on earth and show us your approval by making our efforts successful for your glory, and may the stories you're writing in and through us be inspiring for others to do the same. Grant us the courage to say, "I will," when you call us, and cover us in your favor and approval, this day, so that all we accomplish is done to the glory of your name. We ask it in Jesus' name, Amen.

John Eldredge says the "most dangerous man on earth is the man who has reckoned with his own death. All men die; few man ever really live. Sure, you can create a safe life for yourself ... and end your days in a rest home babbling on about some forgotten misfortune."[10] We're called to participate full out in this life and we're invited to wholeheartedly seek God and the dangerous adventure that He has waiting for each of us. Those who regularly step out by putting their faith into action soon realize that there really is an all-powerful, all-knowing God who is cheering them on and ready to rescue once they "let go" and fully trusted the call that God had placed on their life. So what are you waiting for? Let go!

Thanks for walking this journey with me. I'd love to hear all about the time(s) you let go and let God direct. Tell me all about your "*right here ... right now*" moment where the living and almighty God (El Shaddai) deeply inspired you to answer His call to let go and the impossible became possible and you put your faith into action and responded with the expectation of a kairos moment when you shouted out loud, "You want me to ... *What?*"

---

[10] Eldredge, *Wild at Heart,* 169.

BIBLIOGRAPHY

"No Risk, No Fun? People Who Take Risks More Satisfied With Their Lives," *ScienceDaily*, University of Bonn (September 19, 2005). http://www.sciencedaily.com/releases/2005/09/050919081143.htm.

"Success A Family Affair? Willingness to Take Risks And Trust Others Are Inherited, Study Suggests," *ScienceDaily* University of Bonn (November 29, 2006). http://www.sciencedaily.com/releases/2006/11/061128140652.htm

Achtemeir, Paul J. General Editor, The HarperCollins Bible Dictionary, (San Francisco: Harper San Francisco, 1996).

Andelaja, Sunday. *Church Shift*, (Lake Mary: Charisma House, 2008).

Bevere, John. *Under Cover—The Promise of Protection Under His Authority,* (Nashville: Thomas Nelson, 2001).

Bolling, Deborah. "Thy Will Be Done?" *Philadelphia City Paper*, December 4, 2003, http://www.citypaper.net/articles/2003-12-04

Breen, Mike and Walt Kallestad. *The Passionate Church, The Art of Life Changing Discipleship*, (Colorado Springs: NexGen, 2005).

Bundschuh, Rick. *Don't Rock The Boat Capsize It—Loving The Church Too Much to Leave It the Way It Is* (Colorado Springs: NavPress, 2005).

Cole, Neil. *Organic Church—Growing Faith Where Life Happens*, (San Francisco: Jossey-Bass, 2005).

Collins, Owen, *To Quote C.S. Lewis*, (Great Britain: Harper Collins Publishers, 2000).

Dallas Willard Interviewed by Andy Peck for *Christianity + Renewal Magazine* http://www.dwillard.org/articles/artview.asp?artid=92, UK, May 2002.

Eldredge, John. *Waking The Dead*, (Nashville: Thomas Nelson Publishers, 2003).

Eldredge, John. *Wild at Heart,* (Nashville: Thomas Nelson Publishers,

2001).

Fiorina, Carly. *Tough Choices—A Memoir*, (New York: Penguin Group, 2006).

Garland, David E. *The NIV Application Commentary, Colossians/ Philemon*, (Grand Rapids: Zondervan, 1998).

Godin, Seth. *The Purple Cow*, (New York: Penguin Group, 2003).

Green, Michael P. *1500 Illustrations for Biblical Preaching*, (Grand Rapids: Baker Books, 2000).

Guinness, Os. *The Call—Finding and Fulfilling the Central Purpose of Your Life* (Nashville: Word Publishing, 1998).

Harrison, R.K. Harrison, edit. *The New Unger's Bible Dictionary*, (Chicago: Moody Press, 1985).

http://transcripts.cnn.com/TRANSCRIPTS/0811/04/cnr.06.html (Nov. 4, 2008)

Jordan, Mary and Kevin Sullivan. *The Prison Angel: Mother Antonia's Journey From Beverly Hills to a Life of Service in a Mexican Jail* (New York: Penguin Press, 2005).

Manning, Brennan. *The Ragamuffin Gospel*, (Sisters: Multnomah Publishers, 2000).

McLaren, Brian D. *The Secret Message of Jesus—Uncovering the Truth That Could Change Everything*, (Nashville: W Publishing Group, 2006).

McManus, Erwin Raphael. *An Unstoppable Force—Daring to Become the Church GOD had in Mind*, (Loveland: Group Publishing Inc., 2001).

McManus, Erwin Raphael. *The Barbarian Way* (Nashville: Thomas Nelson Inc, 2005).

Mounce, William D. *Mounce's Complete Expository Dictionary of Old and New Testament Words*, (Grand Rapids: Zondervan, 2006).

Northcutt, Wendy, *The Darwin Awards—Evolution in Action (*New York: Plume – The Penguin Group, 2002).

Ortberg, John, *If You Want to Walk on Water, You've Got to Get Out of the Boat,* (Grand Rapids: Zondervan Publishing House, 2001).

Ortberg, John. *The Life You've Always Wanted*, (Grand Rapids: Zondervan, 1997).

Pierce, Chuck D. and Rebecca Wagner Systema. *When God Speaks*, (Ventura: Regal Books, 2005).

Reason, Cynthia. "Humber's Operation First Contact a success after students talk to astronaut", *Toronto Community News*, February 3, 2009, http://www.insidetoronto.com/Article/63187.

Rykin, Leland, James C. Wilhoit, Tremper Longman III, General Editors, *Dictionary of Biblical Imagery*, (Downer's Grove: IVP Academic a division of InterVarsity Press, 1998).

Seay, Chris and Brian MacLaren, *The Dust Off Their Feet,* (Nashville: Thomas Nelson Inc., 2006).

Sittser, Jerry. *The Will of God as a Way of Life*, (Grand Rapids: Zondervan, 2004).

Smith Sr., Fred. *Breakfast With Fred*, (Ventura: Regal Books, 2007).

The Canadian Press, "Humber students make contact with Space Station," The Toronto Star, February 2, 2009, http://www.thestar.com/Article/581041.

Tolkien, J.R.R. *The Lord of the Rings: The Fellowship of the Ring* (New York: Mifflin Houghton Company, 1954).

Wall, Robert W. *The New Interpreters Bible Commentary, Volume X* (Nashville: Abingdon Press, 2002).

Walsh, Sheila. *Extraordinary Faith*, (Nashville: Nelson Books, 2005).

Wilkinson, Bruce. *The Dream Giver*, (Sisters: Multnomah Publishing, 2003).

ABOUT THE AUTHOR

Norm Grant has an extensive background in commercial real estate sales, where he earned the title of vice president with one of the largest commercial real estate brokerage companies in the world. Yet at the height of this success he left it all behind to pursue the dream of owning a golf course. Eventually he purchased land to build his dream and then the unexpected happened ... God called. His unreached background set the stage for this strong-minded and religiously skeptic personality to have a very powerful encounter with God. Since then he has walked away from his dream, gone back to school to earn a Master of Divinity from Knox College, University of Toronto, and he now focuses his energies and passion on affecting life change through the spoken word of God.

You're invited to join the conversation by sharing your right here ... right now moments at www.normgrantministries.com.

If you're interested in having the Author speak to your organization or group please email: lifechange@normgrantministries.com.

Additional copies of this book can be purchased at www.normgrantministries.com